I BELONG
GLASGOW

(A journey through care)

Helen Tennent

DEANTAG PRESS
EDINBURGH

This edition published by Deantag Press
6 Nelson Street
Edinburgh
EH3 6LG
Tel: 0131 557 2803
email: deantag@quik.com

ISBN-13: 978-0-9554171-0-8
ISBN-10: 0-9554171-0-4

British Library Cataloguing-in-Publication Data
A catalogue record for this book is available from the British Library

Printed and bound by Metro Press, Edinburgh

F O R E W O R D

In September 1939 my elder sister Meg and I took separate evacuee trains out of Glasgow. I was two and a half years old and she was six. I did not know it then but sixteen years were to pass before I would be permitted to shake off the protective but restrictive chrysalis of the State.

This book tells the story of those years. I have told my story as simply and as honestly as I can. Any inaccuracies are the result of the passage of time but I am sure my readers will forgive me if I have written an incident occurred in May when in fact it took place in June.

For those whose spirit was
crushed beyond repair
and in memory of
Willie and Jeanie Milne of Culantyre
who caught me just in time.

Helen Tennent

ACKNOWLEDGEMENTS

Illustrations numbered below are the copyright of the Mitchell Library, to whom I am indebted for their assistance in tracing the relevant photographs.

Frontispiece, Illus. Nos. 2, 7, 10, 11 and 13.

I would like to record my indebtedness to Alister Chisholm of Inverness, who kindly gave me the following photographs of Jeanie and Willie Milne –

Illus. Nos. 3, 5 and 6.

CONTENTS

Chapter 1	Fresh Fields	7
Chapter 2	Pastures New	19
Chapter 3	Diversions	35
Chapter 4	Nightmare Journey	43
Chapter 5	Highland Ways	49
Chapter 6	Crossroads	75
Chapter 7	Wrong Turning	89
Chapter 8	Lay By	95
Chapter 9	Cul De Sac	103
Chapter 10	Last Lap	113
Chapter 11	Journey`s End	127

1

CHAPTER ONE
Fresh Fields

Although born in 1937, my life, as I remember it, began the day a lady dressed in an olive-green uniform took me away from my parents. It was September, 1939, and I, along with hundreds of my contemporaries, was being evacuated from industrial Glasgow to much safer and healthier climes. My destination was Cove, a small seaside resort nestling on the banks of the River Clyde, where, along with some thirty or forty toddlers under the age of five, I was to spend the next two years sheltering from the horrors of the Second World War. My elder sister Meg, being all of six years, was too old to accompany me and was evacuated on the same day to Perth.

On that Saturday morning, mother bathed Meg and me in the large china sink in the kitchen before dressing us in our Sunday best. When I asked who we were going to visit, she glanced at father. "You tell her," she said in a strange, wavering voice.

He called me over and I climbed on to his knee and listened quietly as he gently explained that we were not going to visit anyone; neither aunts nor cousins. Instead, a nice lady was coming to take Meg and me to live in the country for a little while, where we would be with lots of other children and have lots of space to play in and lots of toys to play with. Because of the war, the government had decided to send all the children out of Glasgow to a safer place. Unfortunately, Meg would have to go to another house miles away, but it wouldn't be long before the war was over and we would all be together again. As he said this, Meg and mother simultaneously burst into tears, but I merely poked my fingers in father's ears and asked, "What is the country?"

With great patience and tenderness, father told me about a land with few houses where strange animals called cows and sheep roamed in grassy fields. During the day they ate the grass and at night, whilst they slept, their bodies turned the grass into wonderful new things. The cows turned it into milk and the sheep into jumpers. He described large trees which reached up to the sky, upon which grew apples, plums and pears; he spoke of magic hillocks beneath which fairies and elves lived in huge, underground palaces; of running water called rivers and large brown birds called hens which laid fresh eggs for breakfast.

So, when the stranger arrived to take me away, I, who had only a puddle-strewn back court in which to play, and who had never seen a cow or a sheep, felt no sadness at leaving behind the room-and-kitchen flat which had been my home for my first two and a half years. I accepted my fate without a whimper. Not even the projected absence of Meg clouded my anticipation of the future now before me. I wanted to go. I wanted to see all those magical things which father had described. A quick hug from my mother, a half crown from my tearful father, a kiss from Meg and I was off, trotting obediently beside the stranger who now held my hand.

Before stepping outside, I let my eyes wander round the dark, dingy flat I was leaving behind. It was a brief, fleeting glance, but enough to leave an indelible imprint on to which I could fasten vague auditory and nasal memories in the years to come. Then with the innocence of my years, I emerged from our old tenement close into the grey, damp daylight of a Glasgow morning with nothing on my mind but the thought that when the sun set that evening I would be squatting underground in a secret cavern supping tea with the Fairy Queen.

Undaunted by the overcast sky, I extricated myself from the outstretched hand of my chaperone and skipped gleefully down the worn tenement stairs towards the waiting black car. This was no exile, no banishment from the city that had spawned me. This was an exciting adventure into the unknown and as I waved my last farewells to Mum, Dad and Meg, I was bubbling over with excitement.

Somewhere between leaving my house and arriving at the railway station, I acquired a round label displaying my name, age and sex, which was pinned to my coat lapel and, presumably for safety, another label bearing the same information, was hung round my neck.

As we moved along the railway platform, I noticed that many of the children waiting for the train were crying, as were some of the adults accompanying them. I found this perplexing. Surely like me they were going to the country and, like me, they should feel happy and excited. Obviously not, and when my chaperone and I reached the peace and seclusion of our reserved railway carriage, I was relieved to learn none of the crying children would be sharing it with us.

I made straight for a window-seat and, after clambering on to it, pressed my nose to the glass, where it remained until the last child had boarded the train. Slowly, noisily, the wheels began to turn, and as if at some hidden signal, the adults left on the platform withdrew handkerchiefs from hidden pockets and began to wave them vigorously at their departing offspring. Within a few minutes the station and the dirt-laden buildings of Glasgow gave way to the green grass and trees of the countryside and I sat still and wide-eyed, fascinated by the changing scenes flashing past the window. I had never seen so much space. I was amazed at how far I could see and, just as Dad had promised, sheep and cows were grazing on the lush green grass. When I could sit still no longer I bombarded my chaperone with childish questions.

"How did the cows get their milk into bottles? Was it true that the sheep made our jumpers? How did they manage to turn the green grass into different coloured wools? Did fairies really live under the ground and, if so, how did they know when it was dark and they could come out to play?"

My 'green lady' smiled and did her best to answer all my questions. As she talked I sat entranced by her clear eyes and her soft voice, particularly her voice. It was so gentle, so kind and all the while I kept wondering why her skin looked so smooth and creamy in contrast to the grey, lined faces of the ladies from my street. At last, my questions answered and my curiosity satisfied, I curled up in my seat feeling safe and secure with my very own 'green lady', closed my eyes and fell asleep.

When I awoke it was in response to the sound of rustling paper. In anticipation of receiving a bag of sweets, I sat upright and glanced across at my companion. I was disappointed. She was unwrapping a long grey box. Nobody carried sweets in such large boxes. Then she said the magical words. "Here Helen, this is for you."

I stared at her for a few seconds then I slid from my seat, crossed the carriage and grabbed the box from her outstretched hands. Without saying a word, I lifted off the lid and there, lying in a mechanical sleep, was the most beautiful china doll I had ever seen.

As I carefully lifted the doll from the tissue-lined box her eyelids fluttered open and two large staring eyes met mine. I gasped in wonderment. After I had stroked my new doll's blonde wavy hair and long brown lashes I looked across at my benefactress. I wanted to hug and kiss her, but instead, lowered my eyes and, as I began exploring my lovely new possession, whispered, "Thank you missus."

She was dressed from head to toe in a yellow woollen outfit, right down to a pair of tiny bootees. When I raised her skirt it revealed a beautiful yellow muslin petticoat, but when I lifted this up I got a surprise. Her panties were white. I looked at them for a moment then, excited by this change in colour, I began to shriek, "Her panties are white. Look, her panties are white." For some strange reason I was unable to understand why they were not yellow. When I had calmed down, we set about choosing a name for her. My chaperone suggested we call her Primrose because my birthday was in April and during that month beautiful yellow flowers of that name grew under large trees in the woods. And so, as the train hurtled towards our destination, my doll was solemnly christened Primrose.

The next memory I have is of being squashed into a car along with some eight or nine other toddlers and being whisked away to a large mansion standing in acres and acres of land. When the car drew up in front of the house all bedlam broke loose. Legs and arms flailed as each infant struggled to be first out of the car. When the mass of waving limbs and screaming heads eventually rolled out in a tangle, I was left a shaken, solitary figure in the back seat, crouched protectively over my Primrose. As soon as I had clambered out, I ran straight to my 'green lady' and held on to her possessively as we climbed the wide steps leading up to the front entrance.

In answer to the loud ringing of the bell, the vestibule door was opened by Matron, a tall, slim lady, dressed in what appeared to be a nurse's uniform. She ushered us into a large, airy room, left us under the supervision of several young nurses, then motioned to my chaperone to follow her. However, not enamoured with the screaming and shouting all around me, I held on to the coat of my 'green lady' in a vain attempt to keep her near me. But my clutching hands were torn away by a pair much larger and stronger than mine belonging to one of the nurses, and my 'green lady' moved unimpeded towards the door. Before reaching it, she turned, smiled at me, then with a wave she disappeared from the room and my life as quickly and as gently as she had entered it.

I was heartbroken, and clasping Primrose to my chest, I joined in the hysterical sobbing reverberating round the room. The nurses made heroic efforts to keep us quiet, but all to no avail. We were not to be consoled. Eventually, they decided we would be more manageable if separated. In pursuance of this objective, a large, dark-haired nurse descended upon me, grabbed one of my arms and dragged me out of the room and across a wide, highly polished hall. I tried to follow as best I could, but this proved somewhat difficult, as she seemed determined my feet would never touch the ground. Up the wide stairs I struggled, trying desperately not to let go my hold of Primrose, and along gleaming corridors and past scores of closed white doors until we reached the one of her choice.

When she unlocked and pushed open the door, my eyes widened in pleasurable astonishment. The room was a veritable Aladdin's cave, crammed full of toys from floor to ceiling. Overawed, I followed nurse into this children's paradise, innocently expecting another present. I stood quite near her stiffly starched apron and let my eyes rove over this hidden hoard of toys. My gaze finally rested on a beautiful doll's house. I moved towards the shelves and was in the process of stretching out a hand to touch the coveted house when I heard a voice say, "Give me your doll, Helen." I froze and looked up at nurse. Two cold eyes peered down at me. I watched her lips move as she repeated her request then I shrank from her in horror.

What did she want my Primrose for? She had enough toys. Surely she couldn't take my lovely doll away from me. I kept my eyes averted as I defiantly whispered, "No, she's mine. The green lady gave her to me." Nurse was not going to be defeated by a mere two-year-old and, with a swift movement, she wrenched Primrose from my arms and placed her on top of a large cupboard where I could never hope to reach her. Then, gripping my hand tightly, she marched me towards the door, apparently oblivious to the hot tears rolling down my cheeks. At the door I twisted round and there my Primrose sat, her large blue eyes staring into space and her little white panties standing out like a flag beneath her rumpled yellow finery. That was the last I saw of her, my first, my most precious china doll. I never did forgive that particular nurse.

When we returned downstairs I joined the crowd of new arrivals for a conducted tour round our new home. Upstairs were the nurses' rooms, the children's dormitories and the bathrooms. Downstairs the ground floor was divided between the kitchen, Matron's suite and the children's quarters. Our side of the house boasted a large dining-room, a main playroom, a smaller playroom and lots of storage cupboards containing outdoor clothes, prams and tricycles.

As I trudged abjectly along the corridors, which were polished to perfection, my overall impression was of how neat and tidy everything was and a horrid thought flitted through my mind. Perhaps we were not allowed to play with anything and had to sit still and quiet all day. However, when the door to the main playroom was thrown open, joy of joys, chaos reigned. Hordes of infants were crawling and running round the room, shouting and screaming at the top of their voices, and toys littered the floor in beautiful disarray.

My relief was short-lived, however, for as I was being introduced to one fat red-faced boy, he picked up one of the large, green, wooden bricks with which he had been playing, and without warning, threw it at me. Fortunately, it missed. True to my Glasgow upbringing, and somewhat annoyed at losing my Primrose, I picked up the brick, rushed towards my attacker and hit him over the head with his own missile. My retaliation had two consequences. I was spanked vigorously and that little boy never threw a brick at me again.

Notwithstanding my unhappy introduction to the playroom, I soon settled down amongst my new companions and was absorbed in my childish world of fantasy when the lunch bell rang. Within seconds the room had emptied of all but we newcomers, who were led to the dining-room and guided to our seat at one of the many long tables. After we were all seated with eyes closed and hands clasped, Matron led us in the saying of grace – a new experience for me. Accustomed as I was to a sandwich of condensed milk and sugar for lunch, the meal was a revelation. Rabbit, vegetables and potatoes followed thick warm soup, and for desert we had a delicious bramble pie. I ate greedily, and when I could eat no more, tripped outside with the rest of the children, happy and contented.

The extensive front lawn stretched down to the banks of the river Clyde, where a huge deer fence stood guard against curious toddlers who might wish to explore the tempting tall grasses and small shrubs lining the riverbanks. To the left of the house, and standing some distance away from it, was a dark and mysterious wood into which numerous small bodies disappeared with alarming rapidity. I was too afraid to enter the wood and plumped instead to play on the front lawn near the house. Toys of all shapes and sizes were brought out for our playtime, and my eyes grew wider and wider as I took in the chutes, the monkey puzzles, the swings, toy prams, tricycles and pointy-head rag dolls.

I spent the whole of that first afternoon sampling all these wonderful toys and as I whizzed up and down the driveway on a small tricycle, my body almost itched with sheer delight. It was a far cry from the brick-strewn back court where I had spent many a day floating match boxes and beer bottle tops in the murky water trapped in holes in the ground. Gone was the grey Glasgow sky. The sun now shone out of a deep blue sky and the fresh air and space simply overwhelmed me. My tireless body, ably supported on two plump, white legs, moved from one newly discovered treasure to another and all the while I kept emitting shrieks of glee.

When the tea bell rang at 5 o'clock, I raced towards the dining-room, my little legs going like pistons. I soon found the seat that had been allocated to me at lunch time and I clambered eagerly on to it. As I sat with eyes closed and hands clasped, I tried hard to concentrate on learning the words of the grace. However, the delicious smell of cooking escaping from the open kitchen door proved too much for me and I almost exploded with relief when I heard the rest of the toddlers say "Amen." The open air and fierce activity had whetted my appetite to an almost unbearable degree and I tucked voraciously into my food. As the boy sitting next to me was homesick and refused to eat anything, I ate his tea as well as my own! When we were given permission to leave the table

I clambered down from my chair and made for the sunny outdoors. But before I could put a foot outside, I was lifted bodily into the air and taken upstairs to join the other children who were being prepared for bed.

At first I was decidedly sulky about the prospect of being bedded at 6 p.m. After all, I was never in bed before 10 p.m. at home, but the gaiety of the nurses and the squeals of delight from the other children as they were teased and tickled mercilessly in the bathroom soon rubbed off on me. Back home I was washed in the kitchen sink and sitting in a bath half-full of warm soapy water was a new and wonderful experience. The luxury of gliding up and down in the bath and splashing water all over me gave me a great thrill and, when my allotted time was up, I was reluctant to leave this large watery playground. However, with so many children to be bathed, my pleas to stay "a wee while longer," were ignored. After I was lifted out, towelled dry and dressed in pyjamas, I was carried shoulder high for a gallop along the corridor to my dormitory.

The dormitory was a long room with huge windows. Twelve beds were lined up against the two longer walls. At the top of the room a white door led into the toilets. Against the bottom wall stood four large white cupboards containing an assortment of clothes, shoes and slippers.

After I had been shown the pot under my bed and told I must use it if I could not reach the toilet in time, I was placed between the cold white sheets, tucked in tightly like a sausage in a beef olive and kissed gently on the forehead by nurse before she disappeared to collect the next bathed tot.

I felt somewhat lost in that large, airy room and as I watched the other children being bedded, I thought of the warm, untidy bed recess in my own home and wondered what my parents and Meg were doing. But strangely, I did not feel too homesick, for I rather enjoyed having a bed to myself. I felt so clean and fresh, not at all sticky and irritable as I had often been when Meg tossed and turned half the night away.

When the last infant in my dormitory had been tucked in, the blinds were drawn and six green lights switched on. I found the green light eerie, and in order to cover my eyes, forced myself lower down in bed, then, exhausted by my day's adventures, I fell fast asleep.

Morning brought an introduction to the daily routine. We were roused at 7 a.m., our beds checked to see if they were dry, then dressed in clean clothes, faces wiped, teeth brushed and hair combed we were allowed downstairs to breakfast. After breakfast we trotted along to the main playroom for free play or organised games. At 12 o'clock we had lunch then, weather permitting, we went outside to play on the lawn. When there was sufficient staff, we were sometimes taken for long walks in the surrounding countryside. I can still remember sitting at the foot of an occupied pram, a large blue floral sun bonnet on my head, being pushed along a tree-lined road by a rather talkative nurse who never seemed to get irritated at my endless stream of questions.

The days slipped past in an endless tapestry of colours and shapes. Meg and my parents disappeared into the background. There was just so much to do and see; slides to go whizzing down, monkey puzzles on which to perform feats of acrobatic daring, tricycles to ride and books and toys in abundance to be explored, including the monstrous, brightly coloured rag dolls with pointed heads, but alas, not my Primrose. The milestones came and went – the first time I dressed myself, the first successful buttoning of my shoes with the aid of a button hook, the tying of my hair ribbon into a neat bow and last, but not least, the ability to read.

During this time certain character traits were forming, amongst which was a deep resentment of regimentation. I got no joy from the innumerable organised games thought up for our entertainment. Wednesday mornings were usually given over to music practice in the small playroom. I was tone deaf and totally disinterested in music. As it was always my luck to get a triangle to wallop or a jew's harp on which to frustrate myself, I eventually decided that I had had enough of music practice and would no longer join the others for this ghastly play hour.

Having made my decision, every Wednesday morning thereafter, I hid behind the heavy curtains in the main playroom and remained there, quite motionless, until all the other children had left the room. As soon as I heard the sound of music coming from the small playroom, I would emerge from my hiding place, extract a few books from the bookcase and retire once more behind the heavy curtains, safely hidden from the eyes of any intruder. Sitting on the wooden window-seat, I slowly and patiently traced over the brightly coloured pages, trying to equate the writing with the pictures. I think it was there, hidden from prying eyes, that my love of books was born. How it happened or at what precise time it came about, I do not recall, but I was an accomplished reader by the time I left Cove at four and a half years of age.

Just as I had decided views about not being regimented, so too had I strong views on friendship. A friend never betrays a friend. I was particularly fond of a little red-haired boy called Brian who occupied the bed next to mine. Unfortunately for Brian he committed the unpardonable – he cliped on me to the nurses.

I must have been about four years old when this incident took place. Although I was expected to use the toilet during the night, I still had a pot under my bed for emergencies. On this particular night I woke from a heavy sleep, slithered down from my bed and made off in the direction of a white gleaming door. Unfortunately, I went the wrong way. Instead of the door leading me into the toilets, it led me inside one of the cupboards at the other end of the dormitory. Still drowsy, I relieved myself all over the shoes, slippers and my pyjamas, which were soaked. When I awoke the following morning my sheets were stained and damp. Panic-stricken and in the vain hope that the nurses would not strip my bed, I pulled up the blankets. However, overcome with the gravity of my misdemeanour, I confided in Brian. Imagine my disgust when at the first sign of the morning nurses, he broke into a chant of "Helen's wet the bed. Helen's wet the bed." I was duly punished with a public spanking but the humiliation I felt was outstripped by my desire for revenge against Brian and I set about achieving it with a wonderful dedication.

From that day on I used my pot every night, and each night lay awake as long as possible hoping to catch Brian going to the toilet. For a few nights I was unsuccessful, but eventually I managed to stay awake long enough to catch him out of bed. As soon as he had disappeared into the toilets I sprang from bed, lifted my half-full pot, rushed over to his empty bed and with one quick movement poured the contents over the bottom sheet before fleeing back to my own bed where I pretended to be fast asleep. When Brian returned he climbed between the sheets and, apparently oblivious to their condition, fell asleep. When morning came I took a vindictive pleasure in reporting him for wetting his bed. He never did question how I knew his bed was wet and he took his spanking with great courage, but never again did I confide in the red-haired Brian,

As my body and my knowledge grew, so too did my imagination. One day we were taken to see a pantomime called Peter Pan. During the performance I was riveted to my seat when Peter sprinkled 'fairy dust' over some of the actors to make them fly. I noticed that the 'fairy dust' came from a cylindrical silvery-blue canister just like the one we had in the bathroom. I left the theatre with only one thought in my head. I too would fly.

The following morning I waited until everyone had gone downstairs to breakfast, then I tiptoed into the bathroom and there, lying on a shelf above the wash basin, was the coveted canister. I grabbed it and made a dash for the landing. Without a moment's hesitation, I emptied some of the white soap flakes into my right hand, sprinkled them over my shoulders and with arms outstretched and heart thumping at the thought of flying into the dining-room, I took off. However, instead of floating gracefully through the air like the actors in the play, I hurtled headlong down the stairs, emitting shrieks of dismay and pain as I bumped and rolled to the bottom of the stairway. Seconds later I was found by a nurse who had been alarmed by my screams. She immediately rushed me along to Matron's office to be patched up.

After listening to my explanation, Matron pulled me towards her. "Really, Helen," she said, "What am I going to do with you?" I turned my tear-stained face towards her and whispered, "Spank me Matron?" She laughed and gave me some sweets for my pains. I think she found my pranks amusing as well as hair-raising.

I was given another opportunity to display my ingenuity the day the doctor came visiting. It was rumoured that we were to be vaccinated, and when a small, plump, middle-aged man arrived and took over Matron's office for this purpose, we lined up in eager anticipation of this mysterious new experience. Naturally, we had no idea what vaccination meant and our queue looked more like a row of tots lining up for ice cream than a crowd of children waiting for a painful jab from a hypodermic needle.

I watched the first boy disappear through the office door, his face flushed with the satisfaction of having beaten us all to the top of the queue. Then I heard it. A long, low whimper followed by screams of "No, no." The chattering and laughing came to an abrupt halt. We stood staring at the closed door. A few seconds later the little boy emerged. Gone was his confident, cheeky smile and instead his face was contorted with pain. I watched him half run, half jump as he made for the front lawn and I wondered why he was clutching his bottom. I watched as the next victim entered the office and when she too came catapulting out clutching at her bottom and voicing sounds of distinct displeasure, my mind was made up. No one, but no one was going to get me through that door.

Terrified, I glanced up and down the corridor searching for an escape route. Salvation was in sight. A little further down the corridor a large wicker laundry basket stood against the wall. Slowly I edged my way towards it, pretending as I did so to skip and dance in an aimless fashion. The other children were too interested in what was going on at the top of the corridor to take any notice of me, and the nurse in charge was too preoccupied with trying to keep them calm to see what I was doing. When her back was turned, I seized my opportunity, snatched open the lid of the empty basket, dived in head first and closed the lid over me. As I sat in the dark with my head resting on my knees, my heart was pounding away so loudly I was afraid someone would hear it.

I remained in my wicker prison until all the children had been vaccinated and the doctor had taken his farewell of Matron. When I was convinced that all activity had ceased and the danger was over, I pushed up the lid, glanced furtively around, then crawled out of the basket and made a frantic sprint for the front door. I was half-way across the lawn before I pulled up. An amazing sight met my eyes. There, lying on their tummies on multi-coloured blankets, were all my contemporaries, their bare bottoms shining like oiled mushrooms in the warm sun. A hum of synchronised sobbing filled the air. Feeling rather conspicuous, I joined a little girl who was lying some distance from the nurses, and I too bared my bottom to the sun, pretending I had been vaccinated. Somehow my ruse went undetected and I felt quite clever at having managed to avoid having my bottom punctured by the dreaded hypodermic!

All this time the war with Germany was in full swing, but with the exception of the barrage balloons fluttering over the Clyde and one night of panic when the bombs dropped too near for comfort, we children were hardly aware that a war was going on.

During my two years at Cove, my parents came to see me at what seemed very long intervals, but they never came together; a fact which puzzled me. Occasionally I would find myself looking at another child trotting between his or her parents and a strange feeling would envelop me, but I never mentioned it to anyone. I doubt very much if I could have put it into words anyway.

By Christmas 1941 my time at Cove had run out. At four years and eight months I was now too old. I was, however, allowed to stay and enjoy the Christmas festivities. My last clear memory of my first home is of standing round a huge Christmas tree in the large front room, singing 'Once in Royal David's City' and watching the candles flutter in rhythm to our breathing. It was a magical, awe-inspiring experience. But here my memory fails, for I do not remember the Christmas Party or the journey back home to Glasgow.

2

CHAPTER TWO
Pastures New

I cannot recall how or with whom I travelled back to Glasgow, but I remember quite vividly my arrival in our street. I had become accustomed to the wide open spaces and cleanliness of the countryside; now as I looked around me I saw dirty, depressing buildings, their stonework blackened and crumbling under the industrial smog of the city. When I entered our close, it seemed damp and airless. However, by the time I reached our front door the excitement at being home overcame any misgivings I may have harboured about the dreariness of my surroundings.

But my memory of home was far removed from reality. When I crossed over the threshold into the hall I was surprised at how small and dark it was. Our kitchen-cum-living room seemed to have shrunk to cupboard-like proportions, and the brown linoleum, cracked from end to end, contrasted unfavourably with the gleaming floors at Cove.

I took in the old familiar objects. The tap still dripped slowly into the cracked china sink. The sagging Rexine-covered chairs in front of the coal fire still trailed their stuffing beneath them. The scarred and somewhat shaky gate-legged table was covered with the familiar white and green checked oilcloth, and screening the bed recess from the rest of the room, hung the yellowing, ageing, lace curtains behind which I had spent many a happy hour playing contentedly with boxes of old buttons.

I ran to the window, expecting to see I know not what, but through the glass there was only one thing to be seen – a tall stone wall, effectively cutting off any view and preventing any sunlight from penetrating into the room. I was craning my neck, trying to look down to where the small drying green should be, when I heard the sound of muffled laughter. I turned, and there, peeping between the lace curtains of the recess, was a vaguely familiar face. I stared at it for a moment. It was Meg. No it wasn't. Yes it was. With a squeal of joy I ran towards her. We hugged and kissed each other enthusiastically. As the evening wore on, however, I found myself glancing furtively at my elder sister. She was so changed that she seemed something of a stranger to me.

That night, however, forced into close contact in our communal bed, her strangeness melted away until at last she did indeed look and talk like the sister I had left behind. We lay awake till very late, exchanging stories of the places we had been and the things we had seen until, exhausted, we fell asleep. However, in response to Meg's tossing and turning, I woke on several occasions sweating and irritable. I thought of Cove and the cool, clean sheets and wished my Meg were not beside me.

As the days passed, Meg and I became aware that something had altered in our relationship. I was much more independent than she would have liked, and I found her too bossy and demanding for my liking. Down in the back court we spent our time aimlessly kicking an old tin can in and out of muddy puddles or scrambling over piles of broken bricks. I felt hemmed in and frustrated and refused to join in Meg's games – much to her annoyance. Relief from the back court was provided by numerous trips to the little shop round the corner for sweets or lemonade, but despite those treats I was bored and discontented.

If Meg and I had changed, so too had our parents. Dad was now working night shift and Mum, accustomed to the freedom our absence had given her, would sometimes leave Meg in charge of me whilst she went out in pursuit of entertainment.

Meg took it all in her stride, thoroughly enjoying playing at the little mother, but I was none too happy with the situation. The first time she made tea for me was a disaster. She had decided to make us fried eggs and I watched with childish admiration as she placed the pan on the gas stove and carefully broke two eggs into it. My admiration waned however when the house began to fill up with smoke and the smell of burning eggs. She had forgotten to put fat in the pan. That night, along with many another child in our street, our tea consisted of two slices of bread spread with condensed milk.

If Meg's attempts at cooking disgusted me, her method of washing my hair terrified me. In Cove I was used to having my hair washed under the gentle, warm spray of the tap hose. Here we had no hot water let alone a hose, and hair washing under the supervision of my elder, but still young sister, proved to be not only a lengthy but rather hazardous procedure. She began by heating a large pan of water on the stove. When satisfied that it was warm enough, she would pour half of the contents over my head and then lather both my hair and face with what seemed excessive enthusiasm before pouring the remaining water over my head. I did not mind if the water was tepid, but sometimes it was very hot – as I said, it was a hazardous procedure.

Apart from Meg's mothering, I had another new experience to contend with. It was quite apparent that mother and father did not get on. This produced an uncomfortable feeling in my tummy, which could only be relieved by escaping from the house to the back court. I could not remain outside all day, however, so I had to learn to put up with the situation. Sometimes the house would ache with sullen silences and then, usually when Dad discovered we had been left on our own, our kitchen would reverberate to the sound of heated and prolonged verbal barrages.

If the noise unnerved me, the aftermath distressed me even more. When Dad had said all he wanted to say, he would disappear into the bedroom, leaving Mum, Meg and me in the kitchen. Mum would then peer at my legs, pronounce them 'dirty' and proceed to scrub them clean – and I do mean scrub. I was placed on the draining board, my legs dangling in the sink while she scrubbed them with a scrubbing brush. She was oblivious to the terror this produced and seemed unable to comprehend that more often than not the 'dirty' marks were bruises gathered while playing in the back court. Sometimes, instead of having my legs scrubbed, she would insist that I was the cause of all her unhappiness, and I would be forced to stand facing a wall reciting over and over again that I was a naughty girl and no one loved me. Fortunately I was rescued from this rather confusing existence by another move.

Sometime in 1942, Meg and I were evacuated once again, but this time together, to the Suncourt Hotel which stood overlooking the sandy beach of Troon. My memories of our stay there are very few. I remember trying to fry birds' eggs on hot rocks; trotting down to the Marine Hotel for handfuls of uncooked macaroni, which was dispensed by the WRENS who were billeted there; going to church and staring wide-eyed at the deep blues and reds of the stained glass windows; marvelling at the lustre of brown, green and maroon tiles lying in a pile at the back of the hotel, and one bizarre incident which took place in my dormitory. I walked in to find one of the girls stretched out on her bed whilst a line of boys of a similar age queued up for the privilege of lying on top of her. They were all laughing and giggling. I could not understand what was so funny or entertaining about their game.

We had only been in Suncourt Hotel for a few months when we were given orders to move yet again. Meg had been allocated a place in a private house in Monkton on the outskirts of Troon whilst I, because of my age, had been allocated a place in Pinwherry which was some considerable distance away. This time Dad put his foot down and insisted we both go to Monkton. The authorities capitulated and, when we left Suncourt, we left together.

As we approached Monkton, I noticed that the houses were much larger and more spaced out than the bungalows near the beach and by the time we reached Glenholm, the house where we were to live, it was apparent that

1. The Former Suncourt Hotel, overlooking the sands of Troon.

we were in a very select area indeed. The driveway was flanked on either side by a red sandstone wall. On one side was a shrubbery and on the other a beautiful wood. As we drove up the driveway we passed several children who smiled and waved at us. When we reached the end of the drive I found myself looking at the most beautiful mansion I had ever seen. The house was large and elegantly proportioned. Balconies sprouted from first floor French windows, their angular outlines softened and enhanced by lush ivy clinging tenaciously to the stonework. This wonderful house belonged to a lady called Mrs. Mackie Campbell, whom we addressed as 'Madame'. Madame lived in one half of the house, whilst some twenty girls and a small staff lived in the other half.

We entered by the conservatory, a large cool room resembling a three-sided shed. The floor was made of cold stone slabs and the walls were lined with green wooden cupboards which, I discovered later, housed the produce of the large vegetable garden to the side of the building. We followed our escort along a narrow corridor to Matron's study. She was a plump, cheerful woman and after she had warned us that at no time were we to wander into Madame's half of the house or her part of the garden, she delegated one of the older girls to take us round our new quarters.

On the ground floor we had the use of the large kitchen, where we were each allocated a cupboard to store our hats, gloves and school satchels. Upstairs I was to share a room with four other girls, whilst Meg was allocated a bed farther along the corridor amongst several of the older girls.

My dormitory looked very cosy and warm. Each bed boasted a highly coloured crocheted woollen cover and a wooden locker. Unlike the stark dormitories of Cove and the Suncourt Hotel, personal possessions littered the lockers and beds, giving the room a lived-in feel. The girls were very friendly, and within hours I struck up a friendship with one of the older girls, Nancy Gunn, who took me under her wing and showed me round the vast grounds and even vaster fruit and vegetable gardens.

At the top of the driveway, on the right-hand side, stood a massive garage housing several lovely cars, now lying idle because of the petrol rationing. Over the garage were two small self-contained flats, which were occupied by the cook, Mrs. Paterson, and the handyman, whose name I forget. At the foot of the driveway, on the left-hand side, lay the wood. After Nancy and I had climbed up the wall bordering the driveway, she led me along a well-worn path to the vegetable garden. As we walked under the leafy trees I found the stillness of the wood most appealing. The ground beneath our feet was a beautiful brown and yielded gently to the weight of our bodies. It was a magical place where, in the right season, large red, white-spotted toadstools flourished. Here indeed I could imagine elves and fairies dancing in the moonlight.

I was totally unprepared for the vegetable garden. It was monstrous. Row upon row of growing plants stretched into what seemed infinity – future potatoes, tomatoes, cucumbers, marrows, and trees laden with budding fruits which would ripen in the autumn into delicious apples, pears and plums. I was suitably impressed.

During our first summer at Glenholm, we spent most of our playtime on the golden sands of Troon, where a flood of new experiences stimulated my every sense. I learned not to pull esparto grass – it fought back and gave you a nasty cut. Not to run barefoot over the sands, for lurking under the smooth surface lay jagged pieces of glass, sharp pointed twigs and, most dreaded of all, rusty tin cans, which had been left behind by careless picnickers. I was taught not to wave at low-flying aircraft but to throw myself flat on the ground whenever one passed overhead. As the aircraft were always our own, I found this a rather tiresome procedure. I also learned to steer clear of the alleged quicksand, where, according to the older girls, several people, including a horse and cart, had disappeared forever beneath its shimmering, treacherous surface.

One skill I did not master, however, was that of swimming. This was no doubt due to Meg's teaching methods. A competent swimmer herself, she found my fear of water incomprehensible and decided to help me overcome it by taking me out beyond my depth and leaving me to make my own way back. It did not work, and even today, despite having learned to swim in my fifties, I have a strong fear of swimming out of my depth.

Apart from that experience, my first summer at Glenholm was filled with days of unadulterated pleasure. I warmed in the sunlight to a golden brown. I guddled at the edge of the water for the ever-elusive crabs. I poked long sticks at poor beached jellyfish and grew cheeky and confident on the love lavished on me by the older girls, who looked upon me as a source of endless amusement.

As the summer holidays drew to a close, signs began to appear that our days of playing on the beach were coming to an end. In the large kitchen our cupboards began to bulge with woollen vests, warm liberty bodices, school hats, gloves and scarves. Excursions were made into town for heavy black shoes which threatened to break your feet first time on, thick nap coats which made you look like a walking bear and school satchels which kept slipping down your arms no matter how often you hitched up the straps.

My first day at school was a bit of a disaster. Most of the infants in my class seemed unhappy, and the tears of those not inclined to favour the discipline reminded me of my first day at Cove. Fortunately our teacher, Miss Faulds, had considerable patience and eventually managed to get us all under control.

I spent my first afternoon at school playing with brick jigsaws, threading coloured square beads on to long laces and cutting out gnomes and Santa Clauses from old Christmas paper. I found scissors the most awkward things, and whilst I was expert at completing the jigsaws and adept at threading the beads, my Santa Clauses were very untidy indeed.

Slowly we progressed to lacing simple shapes on pre-pierced cardboard, counting thin slivers of purple, green, red and yellow wood and adding up dots on pieces of paper. Finally the day arrived when we were given our first reading book and a brown folder containing all the tables. I could hardly wait to get home to show Meg my new possessions. That night I diligently learned my first page of formal reading by heart. "Run Rover run. See Rover run. Rover catch the ball. Well done Rover." Before the class had finished the book I had practically learned it off by heart and was pleased when we moved on to another about Tittie Mouse and Tattie Mouse.

I was in my element at school and thoroughly enjoyed my lessons. No doubt some of my enthusiasm was due to my attachment to Miss Faulds. When that gentle soul learned I was an evacuee she took it upon herself to provide me with two slices of buttered toast for my morning playpiece and thereby earned my undying devotion. This kindness urged me on to greater and greater endeavours to please her, and by the time I was seven years old I was reading "The Red Letter" and "The Silver Star" – romantic magazines which I scrounged from Meg. Whilst the content of my reading matter may not have met with Miss Faulds approval, my prowess at reading did.

If I was studious and obedient in the classroom, I was a positive tomboy during the lunch hour. What I did with that hour depended largely on whether or not we got a sponge pudding for dessert at lunchtime. If it was sponge pudding, my chum and I would lick off the custard adhering to the green or white icing, hide the sponge under our cardigans and, as soon as we were outside, run as fast as our legs would carry us to a little shop in the centre of town which was used by the Red Cross. In the waiting room, the shelves of which were stacked with a variety of books, I would read poetry aloud from a large book of Nursery Rhymes to whoever was on duty. I spent many a happy lunch hour in that little shop, nibbling my sponge and sipping warm tea from a delicate china cup.

On those days when no sponge appeared, I threw ladylike habits to the wind, and my chum and I would make for the nearby railway line where I thrilled her with feats of acrobatic daring or stupidity, depending on one's point of view. I can still remember swinging by my hands beneath the girders of the railway bridge until my friend pleaded with me to return to the safety of the railway embankment. When I look back on those escapades, I shudder to think what would have happened if I had lost my grip and plummeted on to the railway lines below.

Meg, of course, was not at the Primary School, but attended Troon High, which catered for children between the ages of seven and eleven. I was very proud of her when she passed her eleven plus at the age of ten and became one of the youngest children to attend Mar College – and this despite the fact she had been forced to spend several days, if not weeks, in isolation without access to books because she had caught impetigo!

My poor Meg. She seemed to be predisposed to illness. If she was not lying prostrate on cold rubber sheets to stop her nose from bleeding, she was dropping down in fainting fits all over the place. I have no doubt that her delicate condition stemmed from the fact that she had an aversion to eating protein foods. Meat and eggs were always passed up in favour of puddings or a jam sandwich. Unfortunately this strange diet passed unnoticed amidst the crowd. I was only aware of it because I consumed what she refused.

When winter drew in, the shorter days forced us into our playroom, which became an amateur theatre for the older girls who put on plays and concerts for our amusement. I have a beautiful memory of a girl called Eileen standing in front of a seated audience of children and staff singing "The White Cliffs of Dover". As she stood, slim and elegant in her mother's emerald green chiffon evening dress, her red hair gleamed under the electric light bulb until it looked as if she had a halo round her head. How much we were affected by the words of the song or the clarity and timbre of her young soprano voice, I do not know, but when she had finished singing there were quite a few tear-stained faces in the crowd. Despite my youth I was not unmoved. A strange new feeling invaded my body. It was an aggressive feeling; a feeling of belonging; of identifying with those around me and of being prepared to defend them to the death. I blushed as this strange emotion, this emergence of patriotism, increased my heart rate and made my body warm.

During the long winter months we paid regular Saturday visits to the local cinema. In the dimmed hall, as I chewed squares of McGowan's chocolate toffee, I sat enthralled as I was entertained by Fred Astaire, Ginger Rogers and Deanna Durbin, not to mention Bob Hope and Bing Crosby. I couldn't understand everything in the Hope and Crosby Road epics, and often their escapades with semi-nude natives or wild jungle beasts would leave me shaking in terror. Here too I saw "Lassie Come Home", the frightening "Madonna of the Seven Moons" and the sad, but haunting "Sullivan Brothers". But it was not those colourful dramas that provided me with my ever-recurring nightmares. It was the newsreels now full of the horrors of the war.

If my nightmares were born in the cinema, they were nurtured by the talk that took place afterwards in our dormitory. As soon as the lights were out my companions would go over everything we had seen in great detail, including the newsreels, and would spend hours devising bizarre methods of killing Hitler. After listening to these tales I would fall into a fitful sleep, only to awake several hours later bathed in sweat, my limbs twitching and my mouth wide open, completely unable to relate to my surroundings. When at last my silent screams escaped, I would fill the dormitory with loud anguished cries of "No, no." In order to stop me from disturbing the other girls, it was decided that I should sleep with Matron, an arrangement that pleased both the girls and me. I loved sharing her bed and when she retired for the night I would secretly watch her combing her long hair in front of the mirror. She looked so soft and cuddly that I would often wish she were my mother and I could sit on her lap and tell her all my secrets and dreams. However, I confined myself to snuggling into her back and permitting myself to be lulled into a deep undisturbed sleep, safe in the knowledge that no-one could harm me while Matron was there, not even

Hitler.

Alas, little girls also have their naughty moments and I took advantage of my special privilege. At regular intervals round the house there were huge grilles to drain away any water that might otherwise lie round the stonework. There, in the summer, frogs and toads would gather to escape the drying heat. When dared to put one in Matron's bed, I rose to the challenge. I spent hours fishing down the grilles and when I finally snatched a large toad I put it in an old shoebox until such time as I could release it. That night, just as Matron was about to climb into bed, I opened the box and let the toad jump out. The sight of this slimy, brown pulsating mass was just too much for her and, despite my abject apologies, I was ordered back to my dormitory.

Apart from our concerts and cinema going, we had another distraction. From time to time Madame's drive would fill up with American soldiers who slept in the grounds for a few nights. As soon as they appeared we would rush down to the gardener and buy small cucumbers and tomatoes, which we would exchange for bars of chocolate with the soldiers.

After a few days' respite, our visitors would pack up their belongings and the drive and grounds would empty as noisily and as quickly as they had filled, and our lives would be a little lonelier and sadder without them. There was, however, a permanent army camp down the road, and although it was out of bounds, Meg and I would often sneak into the camp through an adjoining field which belonged to a local, retired Colonel. In the warm kitchen, cook would treat us to large helpings of delicious apple and blackberry pie.

One day, as we were sauntering home through the delicate white and lilac Mayflowers happily munching on a piece of pie, we heard a terrific roar. It was the Colonel, gun slung menacingly over his arm. We took off as one. I reached the loose wooden paling in the fence first, but in my panic, got stuck. Meg, having no desire to be caught, and alarmed at the time I was taking to crawl through the small opening, decided to hasten her exit by jumping over the fence. Unfortunately, she landed on top of my emerging body. Bruised and shaken, we disentangled ourselves, and without a backward glance made for home and safety, leaving the irate Colonel master of his empty field.

During our stay at Glenholm, Meg formed a very strong attachment to Madame Mackie Campbell and often visited her part of the house to help her dress and to arrange her hair for dinner. Although she told us of the beautiful evening dresses Madame wore and the elegant guests who came to dinner, she never revealed what she and Madame talked about. This was her private world, and in a way I understood why she wanted to keep it hidden from the rest of us. She, much more than I, felt the need to confide in an older person and in Madame she had found someone who would listen to her girlish secrets.

As a result of Madame's friendship with Meg, I was occasionally treated to trips into town with them. As Madame did not appear to use any money, presumably using charge accounts, in my innocence I thought she owned all the shops in Troon. Sometimes, in the summer, when Madame's family or friends were visiting, Meg and I would join them on the beach to picnic on wafer thin cucumber sandwiches, strange sweet pastries and fiery-red lobsters. I always refused to eat the latter – I found the look of their hard crusty bodies repulsive. Besides, the thought of boiling any creature alive appalled me.

We maintained our link with home through Dad's none-too-frequent visits. He always arrived smiling and cheerful, his bonhomie largely attributable to the prerequisite wee dram. After handing over our presents of sweets and fruit, he invariably made for the beach to collect winkles for his tea. I detested the sight of these slimy looking creatures, but as long as they remained tightly curled up inside their shell, I reluctantly collected them in a paper bag for Dad, who obviously looked upon them as a delicacy.

Mum only visited us once. At least I can only remember one visit. On that memorable day, a never-before-seen-or-heard-of Uncle John accompanied her. As soon as Meg clapped eyes on him, she became sullen and withdrawn. I, as usual, followed her example and refused to speak to this stranger. Mum, quite put out by our silence, decided I was a mess, and hauled me upstairs to wash my face and cut my hair. I felt a little put out at this, particularly as I had spent a lot of time preparing myself for her, and my lower lip began to protrude ominously. It protruded somewhat more when I realised our day out was to be financed with the pocket money Meg and I had saved for special occasions.

It was a disastrous day and I was relieved when it came to an end. When they finally departed, Mum requisitioned a lot of my lovely clothes, which she claimed were too small for me. Meg retired to her dormitory to cry, and I, unable to understand why, ran out to play in the dying rays of the sun, thankful that I would not have my legs scrubbed that night. A few days later, Meg told me Mum and Dad had separated for good. I was too young to understand what separated meant and thought Mum had been evacuated from Glasgow.

As 1944 drew to a close, rumours began to circulate that we would be going home for Christmas. When Matron confirmed the rumours were true, we threw ourselves into hectic preparations for our last concert. Madame threw an extravagant party in her marble-tiled reception hall, decorating it with a profusion of greenery and glittery ornaments.

The airmen stationed at Prestwick organised a going home party for all the evacuees in the area. In order that I should look my best on this splendid occasion, I was introduced to the painful process of hair curling. I didn't mind sitting still for hours as Meg wound strands of my short hair round long strips of cloth. However, when they were removed the following morning with half my hair entwined around them, I was less than enthusiastic with the results, for my shiny hair now looked dry and frizzy.

I had one party dress – a lovely blue, frilled satin concoction with mother of pearl buttons and a wide, pink satin waist ribbon. However, my heavy black school shoes looked incongruous with the dress. When Madame heard of my plight, she rushed me down town and bought me a beautiful pair of dance shoes. When I slipped the soft, black leather over my feet I felt my toes tingling with the sheer luxury of the feel of the light and flexible material. Without a trace of self-consciousness, I skipped, danced and pirouetted all round the house showing off my lovely, my first pair of pom poms to anyone who looked at them.

On the night of the party, we were driven to Prestwick in a fleet of taxis, but as the camp was in complete darkness we had some difficulty finding the main hall. Eventually we knocked on the right door and gained admission to the brightly lit, but heavily curtained hut, which was already half full with children.

A tall quiet man called Jim took Meg and me under his wing and after we had demolished our Christmas dinner – served in a compartmentalised aluminium tray – he took us on a tour of the camp. This was strictly forbidden, but the fact that we had to keep very quiet as we crept stealthily from one hut to another, only made the experience more exciting. In each hut, I recited a poem and performed an amateurish dance for the occupants, and in response to their questions, I gave them a stream of childish nonsense. In return, they rewarded me with profuse gifts of sweets, which Jim collected in a large cardboard box. Meg, always much quieter than I, refused to perform despite repeated cajoling. We were returned to the main hall in time to welcome Santa Claus who, I noticed, wore trousers just like the airmen under his voluminous red robes. We each received a carrier bag full of presents, which Matron immediately took from us and placed in the waiting taxis. But the gift that gave me the most pleasure was the one Jim handed to me. It was a small china doll dressed in a black and red Hungarian outfit with a beautifully embroidered apron. As I looked at her, I thought of my other china doll, my beautiful lost Primrose and I determined no one would take this one from me. I did manage to hold on to her, my last doll, until she practically disintegrated under my constant stroking.

The following few days were chaotic. We were all far too excited to sleep and discipline broke down.

On the day of our departure we were up at dawn, checking our packed cases and exploring the carrier bags which Matron had placed at the foot of our beds. Apart from a box of shiny, perfumed, striped sweets, the only present I remember was a necklace made of shells so delicate that when you held them up to the light you could see through them. These I donned over my thick nap coat before following the rest of the girls to the foot of the drive to wait for the bus.

It had been snowing the previous night and all the shrubs were covered in a fine coating of snow, which glistened and sparkled in the weak morning sun. While waiting for the bus to arrive, we sang the following song over and over again -

They say there's a ship just leaving Bombay
Bound for old Glasgow's shore
Heavily laden with wee evacuees
Bound for the land they adore
So pack up your cases
And wash all your faces
You're bound for the land you adore.

I was sitting on the red sandstone wall watching my friend Nancy drawing in her sketchbook when I got the first indication that something was wrong. Matron suddenly appeared at the top of the drive and called out Meg's name. I watched my sister walk slowly up the drive towards her. When they disappeared into the house, I felt the first shiver of apprehension.

When Meg re-appeared a few moments later, although she was half-running, half-walking, it seemed as if she was moving in slow motion. Her face was drained of all colour and her eyes were red from crying. Long before she reached me I heard her words float through the cold, still air. "We're not going Helen. We're not going home." All chattering ceased. All eyes turned towards her. For a moment I thought this was one of her mischievous tricks. But a long glance at her tear-stained face told me this was no trick. In between her anguished sobbing, she blurted out that Dad could not take us home until he had found someone to look after us. I was stunned. What did she mean? Where was mother? Confused and alarmed at Meg's distress, I clung to Nancy, buried my head in her warm neck and cried as I had never cried before. Nancy tried desperately to console me, to reassure me that it would not be long before I followed the rest home. By the time I had pulled myself together, Meg had fled up the driveway and disappeared.

When the bus finally arrived, the girls who had crowded around me in support moved away and climbed silently inside. I gave Nancy a last hug. For a few moments our eyes met, then she too moved away and entered the bus. The large doors closed. I stood at the gateway, a forlorn little figure, shrouded in my warm black coat over which lay my now forgotten beautiful shell necklace. As the bus moved off, I waved at the faces peering out of the back window and I kept on waving till the bus and its occupants disappeared from my sight.

Gone. They were all gone. The friends who had given me so much pleasure and who had guided me through my most impressionable years. I felt the cold wind pierce my coat. The tears fought for release and then jumped from my eyes and bumped and slid down my burning cheeks. It wasn't possible. It was a nightmare. I nipped myself on the back of my hands, but despite the pain, still clung to the hope I was dreaming. I turned and looked up the empty driveway. The snow lay like a diamond-studded ermine over the grey gravel. How could such beauty exist side by side with such sorrow. In a trance, I stared at the driveway for a few moments longer then my tears stopped flowing. Slowly, deliberately, I walked up that side of the drive unmarked by our play and when I reached the top, I turned and looked at my footprints. No, this was no dream. These were my tracks. I felt my body flush hot and cold from head to toe. Now I knew what separation meant. We were alone my Meg and I and life would never be the same.

When I returned to the house I searched high and low for Meg. I found her sobbing in Matron's arms. I tried to comfort her by patting her on the back and uttering "There, there," but she would have none of it, my poor, poor Meg. At the age of seven I could not possibly know the ache which was consuming her, or the fears her extra knowledge fuelled. I was heartbroken, of course, but Meg's sorrow was painful to watch. She spent the rest of the day curled up on top of her bed giving vent to the most dreadful sobbing that I hated my parents for letting her suffer so.

During the following days, when Meg was not lying on top of her bed, we wandered aimlessly from room to room, helping the remaining nurses strip the beds which were now no longer needed. When this task was completed, the majority of the remaining nurses also disappeared and we felt more lonely and isolated than ever.

Outside we were lost. In place of our former loud and boisterous games, we were reduced to walking up and down the driveway kicking mindlessly at the gravel. If I found the daytime boring and lonely, the nights were even more distressing. We were put in a small room where we were surrounded by beds stripped down to the bare springs. Meg could not sleep and I was forced to stay awake as she lived and re-lived fantasies about our parents. She tried to convince me that soon, very soon, Mum and Dad would be reunited and come to collect us. I would agree with her, not because I believed it but because I wanted to go to sleep. It was all falling into place. I looked back at the only visit mother had made to Glenholm and realised, no matter what the reason, we were not an essential part of her life.

After about a week of this sterile existence, four other children who, like us, had been left behind when the exodus to Glasgow had taken place, joined us. They too were depressed and withdrawn, and I found their presence more of an irritant than a relief. I longed for my friends and our cheerful games, but I was learning in that deepest part of the mind where no one intrudes, that longing desperately for something does not guarantee your desires will be granted.

The arrival of the other children seemed to unnerve Meg and she began to behave rather oddly towards me. If I did or said anything to upset her, her right eye would narrow down to a slit and I would then be hauled along to the bathroom where, behind the locked door, I was ordered to stretch out my leg in order that she may repeatedly kick me on the shin. Needless to say, this terrified me, and I would promise to give her the little white bunny which Madam had bought for me if only she would stop. Little white bunnies however hold no great fascination for eleven-year-old girls and my pleadings were ignored.

The next part of my body to arouse her interest was my head. On several occasions I was placed on the low wall lining the driveway in order that she might push me off it until my head bled! Despite my efforts to avoid cutting my head by jumping backwards just as she pushed me, she eventually succeeded in drawing blood. Fortunately the sight of my bleeding head frightened her just as much as it did me, and this game was abandoned.

Her ‘poison’ joke was the most terrifying game of all, particularly as I got no warning before it was played. From time to time she would appear from nowhere carrying a bowl containing a creamy white mixture which she insisted was a poison I had to eat now. After thrusting several spoonfuls of the foul-tasting mixture into my mouth she would then order me to start walking home to Glasgow. At the age of seven I had no idea where Glasgow was let alone how far away it was from Troon. However, as Meg assured me that if I reached Glasgow in two hours time I would not die, I made off towards the main road to Ayr as fast as my legs would carry me. Fortunately I never did have to walk to Glasgow. I was always called back. Only when one of the new arrivals told me the mixture was flour and water did Meg abandon this form of amusement. I’m not a psychologist but upon reflection it looks as if her disappointment at being left behind was being worked out on me.

Some six or seven weeks later, father came to collect us. He looked very old and tired and his voice was unusually flat. He no longer had our old room-and-kitchen. He was now living in digs. But he promised that as soon as we arrived in Glasgow he would find somewhere for us to live.

And so we took our farewell of Glenholm, trotting trustingly beside our Dad who had nowhere for us to sleep.

3

CHAPTER THREE

Diversions

Our search for a new home began at the small attic flat of one of father's old acquaintances, but someone who was a stranger to Meg and me.

When Dad knocked on the door, the lady of the house greeted him like an old friend. When we walked into the small hall, a strange, sickly smell almost overwhelmed me; the source of which became apparent when we trooped into the kitchen-cum-living room. In an old, torn, brown leather chair facing the black range, lay the man of the house, sprawled in a semi-conscious state, half snoring, half moaning. Beside the chair lay a chipped aluminium basin, the contents of which didn't bear investigation. He was obviously suffering from a fierce hangover. Despite his nervous wife's repeated attempts to stir him from his drunken stupor, he remained oblivious to our presence.

Dad and the thin, haggard-looking woman then disappeared into the other room whilst Meg and I sat on a blanket-covered bench. I was disgusted with the squalor of the place, and when my eyes wandered up to the small skylight, through which even the light appeared reluctant to venture, I felt nauseous. Hanging from the ceiling were three flypapers encrusted with an assortment of decaying, winged bodies. As it was winter, they must have been there for months. Surely Dad wasn't going to leave us here?

Time passed slowly, and when Dad returned to the kitchen and said, "Let's go kiddies," Meg and I hastily made for the door. Outside, even the soot-laden wind gusting through the grime-covered close seemed like a breath of fresh air. But although the cloying, sickly smell was soon blown from my nostrils, the feeling of distaste for that place and the hapless couple in it remained with me for a long, long time.

Our next stop was George Square in the centre of the city. Dad left us playing on a patch of green grass before disappearing through the pillar-fronted door of a nearby building. He re-appeared sometime later, looking pale and distracted. When he took us for a fish and chip lunch he seemed to relax a little. Sometimes, however, when his eyes met mine, I saw a look of quiet desperation in them and tongues of apprehension began nibbling at my head and stomach. Apparently he had gone for help to one of the welfare bodies who had advised him to put us into care. At that time, of course, I was unaware of this quick solution to Dad's housing problem.

Our meal over and our bodies recharged, we began our long trek round Glasgow in search of somewhere to sleep, even if only for one night. We climbed up and down never-ending flights of stairs only to have doors shut kindly but firmly in our faces. As darkness descended, so too did the rain and my lovely white ankle socks became spattered and spotted, like the smudged markings of a young tiger. From time to time, Dad left us outside a café while he asked the proprietor for the names and addresses of people who might give us temporary shelter, but without success. Whilst he was making these enquiries, Meg and I huddled together on top of the green glass blocks inserted in the pavement. It was not the colour of the glass that fascinated us, or the dull light shining through it – we had quickly learned that on a cold, damp night, warm air percolated through the glass and kept you from shivering from cold and tiredness.

As the night wore on, my legs began to tire and Meg started to display signs of extreme irritability. I resented the fact that I was not in my warm bed at Glenholm and felt annoyed with Dad for not making sure we had somewhere to sleep before he had collected us. Fortunately, before we broke down altogether, a door opened long enough to let us slide over the threshold.

Our benefactress was a plump, blonde widow, who felt that two more children added to her five for one night would present no problems. Within a few minutes she presented us with a large pot of tea and a plate of succulent bacon sandwiches. When she refused Dad's offer of money, he was so overcome by her kindness that large tears rolled down his haggard face.

As we tucked into our sandwiches, the widow prepared two makeshift beds on the floor, and by the time Dad was ready to go, Meg and I were wrapped in grey woollen blankets and half asleep. Dad came to collect us early in the morning and when the widow again refused payment for her kindness, Dad gave half-a-crown to each of the children. After thanking her again, we returned to the streets full of optimism that today might bring us a more permanent home.

We spent the morning going back and forward on green and yellow trams till Dad found someone who gave him the name and address of an acquaintance, a Mrs. McDonald, who might take us in. Following this lead, we hopped on a bus that took as to the suburb of Knightswood. The area looked clean and respectable and when we finally reached the correct address I happily noted that the close was fresh and tidy.

In response to Dad's knock, the door was opened hesitantly by a thin, elderly lady. She listened attentively, if not a little suspiciously, as Dad explained his position. When he had finished talking, she grunted, glanced down at Meg and me, and then stared vacantly into space. After what seemed an eternity, she gave another grunt, opened her door wide and invited us in.

Meg and I sat in the armchairs in front of the glowing kitchen range while Mrs. McDonald discussed the financial aspects of looking after us. It was so cosy and warm that I had difficulty staying awake. Meg on the other hand, sat straight-backed and very serious-looking on the edge of her chair.

Eventually a bargain was struck. Mrs. McDonald agreed to take us in. As it was only a room-and-kitchen flat, this meant Mrs. McDonald would have to share her bed with her 13 or 14 year old granddaughter Morag, while Meg and I shared the bed in the kitchen recess. The matter settled, Dad made his farewells and rushed back to work to make up for lost time.

As soon as the door had closed behind him, Mrs. McDonald brought out a box of Morag's old toys to occupy us till teatime, when we helped her make a massive quantity of thick chips. I discovered in the days that followed that, apart from the occasional egg or piece of fish, chips formed a major part of Mrs. McDonald's diet. Not that I found this a less than adequate diet – I had no knowledge of proteins or vitamins. If chips were good enough for Mrs. McDonald and half of Glasgow's population, then they were good enough for me.

After tea, Meg and Morag went out to play in the street while Mrs. McDonald and I settled in front of the fire. A captive but entranced audience, I sat beside Mrs. McDonald and listened attentively to tales of long ago when she was a young and beautiful lady. Such tales – tales of large mansions and well-to-do gentlemen, all of whom had apparently proposed to her. I liked the sound of those tales. Perhaps well-to-do men would propose to me and I would live in a lovely mansion and never again need to walk the streets looking for a home. I asked Mrs. McDonald if she thought such men as she described would want to marry me. She replied, "Keep yourself nice and clean and handsome, rich young men will propose to you." The idea pleased me and I warmed to this talkative lady, who rose even higher in my estimation when she let me wash myself – no horrible leg-scrubbing here.

Our first night behind the kitchen recess curtains was almost like being back home, except the atmosphere was more relaxed. I felt happy that I wouldn't need to tramp the streets tomorrow and keep my eyes lowered as Dad pleaded with strangers to take us in. Tomorrow, when I went to play in my new neighbourhood, I could look all the other little girls in the eye, for I too had a bed to sleep in and a lovely coal fire to keep me warm. With these thoughts swishing round in my head, I fell into a deep sleep. Unfortunately the experiences of the last two months had taken their toll on Meg, and my sleep was repeatedly disturbed by her frenzied prodding and nipping, for she was determined I would not sleep whilst she was awake. It didn't take long for Mrs. McDonald to notice what Meg was up to and within a week I had changed places with her granddaughter.

Mrs. McDonald and I got on very well together. When her housework was finished she would let me try on her beautiful satin and chiffon evening dresses – each one of which had a romantic tale attached to it. My favourite dress was made of heavy cream satin patterned with tight pink rosebuds and sporting a magnificent bustle. I was forever marching up and down in this beautiful gown with my feet stuck into high-heeled shoes that were several sizes too big for me. From time to time I was even allowed to wear Mrs. McDonald's wedding dress. From the quality of her beautiful clothes, it seemed probable that at some time she may have enjoyed a more affluent way of life and that a few of her tales had an element of truth to them.

One of her tales, however, was not so amusing. It centred round an unfortunate neighbour. It seems this lady, believing that she was going blind, decided to end her life and jumped from her second floor bedroom window. Much to her chagrin, instead of going to meet her Maker, she merely managed to break all four of her limbs. "Says she wouldn't have done it if she knew what was going to happen," Mrs. McDonald would mutter as she pulled her black shawl around her. "Now she's covered in Plaster of Paris." When she came to this part of the tale she would sometimes break down at the thought of her neighbour's predicament. On other occasions, she would be convulsed with laughter as she pointed out the exact spot where her neighbour had landed. I was horrified at the idea of this poor woman being covered in what Mrs. McDonald assured me was a cement-like substance, and each night I prayed to God to break the Plaster of Paris and set the poor woman free. I even went so far as to suggest to him that perhaps the lady had not intended to kill herself but was merely trying to fly like I had been trying to do when I fell down the stairs at Cove. There was a postscript to this tale – the neighbour had not been going blind, she had merely needed a pair of glasses!

About a week after being deposited with Mrs. McDonald, I was introduced to my first Glasgow school, where I learned more outside than inside the classroom. Meg had been allocated a place in the nearest secondary school. I now found myself in a new environment surrounded by strangers who appeared to adhere strictly to the dictum that only the fittest survive.

My first clash came at the ll o'clock break. In order to avoid being run down by a group of girls stampeding towards me, I stepped backwards and accidentally trod on the feet of a girl standing behind me. I heard a scream and turned round to apologise. Before I could utter a word, I was almost felled by the punch thrown at me by the owner of the unfortunate feet. I didn't take too kindly to this and made my feelings clear. Irritated by my somewhat refined accent, and under the delusion that I was a 'softie', my attacker immediately grabbed me by the hair and dragged me into one of the many brick shelters dotted throughout the playground. I was in no doubt as to what she intended to do. Despite the panic convulsing my body, I gave as good as I got and it was she, not I, who left the shelter with a bleeding nose.

As I sauntered home after my first day at school, I didn't have a care in the world. Not until I heard a loud voice shouting, "There she is. There's the smarty pants." I turned round to see what poor mite was going to get it. When I spotted my erstwhile sparring partner with a crowd of her mates I realised the poor mite was me.

Fear gave me wings. I sped off down the road, my short muscular legs pumping heroically beneath my equally muscular body. When I reached the railway bridge leading down to the main road, I realised that unless I moved faster my pursuers would soon catch up with me. In a desperate attempt to throw them off, I decided to cross, not the bridge, but the railway line which ran along the back of Mrs. McDonald`s tenement. I slithered down to the tracks, hared across the lines, scrambled up the wall and jumped into our back yard. Not until I reached the back entrance to our close did I slow down. By this means I managed to elude my pursuers for some considerable time. Eventually they stopped chasing me and I assumed they had lost interest in me. Not so. One night as I entered the close by the front entrance I spotted several figures emerging from the shadows of the back close. I recognised the all too familiar outlines of my enemies.

With a yell, I tore up the stairs with five girls in pursuit. At the second landing, four remained behind but the tallest kept going. When I reached our landing on the top floor I frantically thumped, kicked and banged on the door. By the time Meg opened it, my pursuer was almost upon me. To my horror Meg would not let me in. After a fleeting glance over my shoulder, she stared into my fear-stricken eyes and hissed, "Smash her," and closed the only escape route in my face. I had no alternative. It was over in minutes and a rather shamefaced girl slunk down to her waiting companions in no doubt whatsoever that, refined accent or not, I was no pushover. I was never troubled again by bullies at that school.

Dad visited us every Sunday and took us for lunch to a nearby café where we were treated to the ubiquitous fish and chips followed by either a McCallum or a Knickerbocker Glory. He enjoyed my tales about Mrs. McDonald, her clothes and her poor misguided neighbour. I think he was pleased that I had settled down well. However, when Meg told him we were fed on a daily diet of chips and cake (an exaggeration on her part) he almost exploded. Our days with Mrs. McDonald were numbered.

This time we moved across the bridge to live in one of the new council maisonettes with Mr. Hamilton, who worked beside father. The Hamiltons were a young and vivacious couple with four children of their own. Although the flat had three bedrooms, it was rather crowded, and there were times when I missed Mrs. McDonald and the personal attention she had lavished on me.

As space was at a premium, Meg and I had to double up with two of the Hamilton children – the two of them sleeping at the top of a double bed, Meg and I at the bottom. This arrangement might have worked out if Meg had allowed me to fall asleep before she did. Unfortunately, if I closed my eyes first she would nip me until I re-opened them. If she awoke during the night and I was sleeping, she would again waken me with her nipping. In a desperate attempt to avoid this, I would wait until she fell asleep then slip quietly from the bed, don my black nap coat over my thin pyjamas and sleep in an old armchair beside the window. It was not the best sleeping place, but at least it was only the cold that awakened me.

I stayed with the Hamitons for several months and yet my memories of that stay are vague and splintered. There were visits to the local Co-op where the floor was covered with sawdust; the buying of groceries which necessitated I memorise a sequence of numbers; glittering beer bottle tops; pancakes covered with sugar and lemon; Mrs. Hamilton curling her hair with tongs heated in the fire and of course that other memory –vague as to who took part or who held the heated poker. Was it a game? I don't know – but whatever it was, I was threatened with the poker unless I fought a boy or boys who were teenagers. Fear, of course, gives you superhuman strength, but did I win or lose – it's a complete blank.

I passed my eighth birthday at the Hamiltons and thought I would live there till I grew up, but the end of hostilities with Germany decreed otherwise. When the war finally drew to a close, young thin men seemed to materialise from nowhere and endless street parties were held to welcome them home. There was a great deal of coming and going and a general air of excitement but, strangely, it was the women whose sons did not return who were the most active. When I realised why, the true meaning of the horrible newsreels I had seen in the cinema at Troon began to make sense. So who were those other people, the ones I watched in the films who lived pain-free, well-ordered lives. They must exist somewhere.

Not long after a big celebration in June, when bonfires were lit and neighbours handed out huge slices of dumpling to the children dancing round the fires, we received a shattering piece of news. Mr. Hamilton had been offered and accepted a job in Coventry. This time there was no trekking up and down tenement stairs. With great reluctance, Dad took us to the Children's Department of Glasgow Corporation in John Street, just off George Square.

I should by now have become accustomed to our moves. This time, however, the impersonal atmosphere of John Street made me feel afraid, not just for what the day would bring, but tomorrow and each day that followed.

As I sat in the highly polished hallway, I nervously poked my fingers into the holes punched out in elaborate patterns on the curved benches. From time to time I glanced anxiously at Dad who was talking through a glass partition to a somewhat officious-looking lady. He seemed to be having difficulty answering questions about our religion. After a bit of discussion, and not a few sighs on the part of the officious-looking lady, we were finally designated Protestants and, the form completed to her satisfaction, Dad joined us on our bench.

We seemed to have been sitting for ages before a small, fat woman strode noisily down the long corridor shouting out our surname. I remember thinking how polite Dad was to her and wondering why he kept calling her "Ma'am". He appeared to be a little overawed by her. She, on the other hand, was full of confidence and pompously curt with him. Dad it seems was no longer in charge. When they had finished talking, she motioned to Meg and I to follow her. The four of us trooped downstairs and out on to the street where a large chauffeur-driven car was waiting for us, that is to say for Meg and me.

Dad hugged us very tightly. As he kissed me goodbye, I felt dampness on his cheeks. We climbed almost trance-like into the back seat of the car. The door slammed shut behind us and the fat lady climbed into the front beside the silent non-smiling chauffeur. Meg and I knelt on the leather seat and peered out the back window towards our Dad, but he had already turned and was walking dejectedly away from us. Nevertheless, we kept waving out the back window until we lost sight of him. But he never looked back. Poor man. He had struggled so hard to keep us together but, despite all his efforts, he had failed. A new era had begun. Never again would we live as family.

4

CHAPTER FOUR
Nightmare Journey

2. Foresthall Hospital, formerly the poorhouse. Now demolished.

There are no words in a child's vocabulary to describe fear of the unknown, so we sat staring out of the car windows, unable to express our thoughts or to comfort each other.

I had no idea how Meg was feeling, as she, like me, remained silent, but I felt as if I was trapped in an invisible glass bubble. Outside the bubble everything seemed normal. Groups of happy, boisterous children clustered round sweet shops. Harassed-looking women darted from shop to shop in search of off-ration 'luxuries'. Old and not so old men, cigarettes dangling from their lips, leaned against accommodating lamp-posts while Union Jacks and bunting fluttered overhead. Inside the bubble the silence was total.

No, there are no words in a child's vocabulary to express how helpless you are to control your own destiny.

About half an hour later, the car stopped in front of a small, grey stone gatehouse guarding the entrance to a huge building. A small, red-faced man rushed out, spoke briefly to the chauffeur, then with an expansive gesture waved us through the gates. As we drove towards the Victorian building my spirits rose. Perhaps this was going to be just like Cove. And why should I be afraid? After all, my five previous resting-places hadn't been too traumatic and I had come to accept that Dad wasn't a live-in Dad. He was a visiting Dad.

I turned hopefully towards Meg. She was looking decidedly uncomfortable. I looked from her to the grounds and back again. It took several seconds before my brain computed what was causing her concern. Despite it being a beautiful sunny afternoon, there were no children to be seen. The only moving figures were old, very old.

When we entered the building a strong smell of antiseptic filled my nostrils. As we were marched along the hospital-like corridors we passed several of the inmates. They not only looked old and worn out, they looked unhappy. Some walked with eyes averted, feet shuffling; some stood still, nervously stroking their clothing, whilst others seemed to be talking to non-existent companions. I felt Meg's hand clutch mine, her grip vice-like.

Before we reached our destination – the office – a thin, bent man approached the fat lady. With tears running down his weathered, wrinkled face, he begged her to get his boots back from the store because the ones they had given him were too small. The fat lady, in my opinion, brushed him aside, as one would swat a fly. As I passed him, embarrassed, I lowered my eyes and hoped he could not see the guilt I felt at being so fit and young but so unable to help him.

I believe this was the moment cold hate introduced itself to the rest of my emotions, for as I walked behind the fat lady I wished God would strike her down dead. But she, unaware that my eyes were guiding God where to strike, kept on going until we came to a door marked "Staff Only". Before disappearing through it, she ordered us to sit on a wooden bench opposite the door. Some time later we were given a bowl of strongly brewed tea, the smell of which I will forever connect with that God-forsaken place.

When the fat lady finally emerged from the office, she handed us over to a lady dressed in what looked like a nurse's uniform. With no explanation as to where we were, or how long we would remain there, she waddled off, leaving Meg and I to trail after 'nurse' as she led us through a maze of corridors to our dormitory. We were given beds side by side. Before she too disappeared, 'nurse' told us we could go out to play till the tea bell rang at 5 p.m. and warned us that five minutes later the doors to the dining-room would be locked.

Unsure of ourselves, we stood beside our beds for about fifteen minutes. Eventually Meg took my hand and led me outside. She headed straight for the gatehouse but the gateman rushed forward and barred her path.

"And where do you think you're going?" he demanded.

"For a walk," replied Meg.

"Have you got a pass?"

"What do you mean, a pass?"

"You need a pass to get out."

"Where are we then?"

"You're in Foresthall, the poorhouse lass," was the unexpected reply.

Meg's rosy cheeks blanched. She took a deep breath, bit her lip and turned on her heels. As we headed back up the drive I asked, "What does the poorhouse mean? Are we going to be locked up here for life?" She explained the poorhouse was for people who were poor and homeless. As she said the last word she burst into tears and ran up the drive, dragging me behind her. We spent the rest of the afternoon clinging to the cold radiators in the dormitory without a single word passing between us.

When the tea bell rang at 5 p.m. precisely, hordes of shuffling bodies swept through the corridors like an ant colony on the march. Mindful of the warning about the dining-room doors being locked against latecomers, we quickly followed and seated ourselves on the nearest empty bench. At five minutes past the hour the two thick wooden doors were closed and locked.

Our fare consisted of a bowl of porridge, a bowl of milk, a plate of soggy, scrambled eggs and two slices of buttered bread. Meg ate nothing. I ate what she refused and when replete, turned my attention towards the other diners.

It wasn't the unfocussed watery eyes of the elderly and demented which filled me with revulsion. It was their skin – skin so thin it could not conceal or contain the tortuous purple blood vessels which bulged and snaked wantonly along the back of their hands until enfolded by the muscles and fat above the wrists. A horrid thought flitted into my head. "Did everyone in here end up like that? Would I end up like them – weak, unwanted and half mad?"

Panic-stricken, I sent up a silent prayer to God, pleading with him to let me stay young just a little longer; to allow me time to play on the grass; grow into a young lady and have a house and family of my own. And as I sat quietly, my hands folded lightly on my floral cotton dress, I could hear my heart pounding out the words, "Are you alive, are you dead, are you alive, are you dead?" But there were no kind eyes to soften at my terror and no listening ears to absorb my fears. When the dining-room doors were eventually thrown open, we fled from that nightmarish room to our dormitory, only to enter another nightmare.

Disturbed by our experience, we stayed in the dormitory till bedtime, when I climbed gratefully between the cold sheets and stretched out stiff as a board waiting for sleep to rescue me. But sleep did not come readily. In the semi-darkness coughs, moans and gentle wails filled the air. Then suddenly all hell broke loose. A flurry of feet, which stopped abruptly halfway down the dormitory. Whisperings, more toing and froing. Two men appeared with an empty trolley. They left with one of the inmates covered by a voluminous white sheet.

The event sparked off a weird conversation.

"Dead."

"Who's dead?"

"Peggy."

"Don't be daft, I was speaking to her this afternoon."

"Listen then, that's her going to the morgue."

I too listened and heard the trolley trundle past the window nearest me.

When comparative silence returned, I lay trying to work out what I had done to end up here. I went over a thousand misdemeanours but could find nothing to warrant this punishment. Eventually I drifted off to sleep only to be awakened by a lady pulling off my bedclothes as she screamed, "Mary come on. It's time to get up." Apparently she thought I was her daughter. After several repetitions of this behaviour, I wrapped myself in a blanket, crawled beneath Meg's bed and remained there until the morning bell assured me it was safe to emerge.

A new day brought new hope. As soon as breakfast was over, Meg and I ran outside and made straight for the gatehouse, but we were again barred from leaving. When we discovered the main building, outbuildings and staff quarters were enclosed behind a tall deer fence and the only way out was through the gate, we gave up and contented ourselves with walking round the large grounds and talking to the old folks.

One of them directed us to a small shop in the grounds where we could buy off-ration sweets. Things were looking up. After buying our sweets we bumped into Agnes. She was a pleasant-looking lady; much younger than the rest and obviously keen to make contact with us. However, as she attempted to communicate with us by alarming gestures and unintelligible grunts, I hid in fear behind Meg till she explained Agnes was deaf and hadn't been taught how to speak.

No longer afraid, I stepped up to her, smiled and offered her a sweet. She smiled back, and after helping herself to a sticky pineapple chunk, stroked my cheeks while large tears gently rolled down her plump face. Over the following days I spent a good deal of my time with Agnes and learned to understand her gestures and grunts. In the months that followed I often thought of her, an anonymous figure, flitting from one low stone wall to another, most at ease with the flowers and insects she adored.

Another lady who left an indelible impression on me was the slim and wiry Mary. She slept in our dormitory and, like Agnes, was younger than most of the other inmates. One day I found her standing outside the main entrance to the building, a small battered suitcase clutched in her right hand. She gaily informed me that her younger sister was coming to take her home.

At lunch time she was still there, not so excited, but still optimistic. Tea time came and went and she was still waiting, but by now she was in an agitated state, marching up and down, endlessly searching the horizon for a glimpse of her sister. Several attempts were made by the staff and the inmates to encourage her to come indoors, but she would have none of it. At seven o'clock she was dragged inside and forcibly put to bed. Her screams as she was held down have stayed with me. I never did find out if her sister had promised to fetch her, but the incident left a very strong impression on my mind. I have no doubt that witnessing it gave birth to my fearful independence, my unalterable belief that it is folly to depend on anyone but yourself.

How long we remained in Foresthall, I do not know. Perhaps a few days, perhaps a week or so, but when the fat lady returned to take us away, I was very glad to see her. Fate sometimes takes funny twists. Years later, when I returned to this nightmarish place, older and much harder, I cocked a snoot at the rules, the ever-watchful gateman and the escort who brought me there. But that story comes later.

Our next destination was a children's home called Auldhouse on the outskirts of Glasgow. Despite the fact that we were with other children, the staff were kind and the food plentiful and delicious, Meg and I had difficulty settling down. Although both staff and children made overtures, we were wary of them and kept ourselves apart. All approaches were met with sullen silence and deep-rooted suspicion. Trusting no one, we closed in on ourselves. At night we refused to sleep in separate beds, choosing despite the warm summer nights, to sleep side by side in a small single bed.

A week or two later we were informed that a home had been found for us on a croft in Inverness-shire and we were whisked off to choose a new wardrobe for our journey. I don't know if the store belonged to the Corporation or whether we were sent to a department store, but when presented with a wide variety of clothes from which to choose our outfits, my sullenness melted away.

When we returned to Auldhouse for our last night, I was animated and talkative but Meg remained quiet and suspicious. That night, however, we slept in separate beds.

Next morning we climbed into the provided car, Meg still quiet and I bubbling over with excitement.

3. The only photo I have of Willie.

5

CHAPTER FIVE
Highland Ways

4. Culantyre as I first saw her.

Accompanied by two jovial male escorts, we travelled by train to Inverness and spent the night in what I think was a small bed and breakfast establishment.

The following morning we were driven some seventeen miles south of the town to Stratherrick, where we were decanted in what seemed to be a large valley of rough grazing ground surrounded by heather-covered hills.

Our companions were a little confused as to which of the many cart tracks leading from the main road would take us to the farm. After some deliberation, they decided to follow the deepest.

As Meg and I plodded over thick green rushes and through peat bogs laced with sweet-smelling myrtle, we cast knowing looks at each other. They were lost these grown-ups and they dare not admit it. However, after we had walked about a quarter of a mile we caught a glimpse of our new home, at least we caught a glimpse of the roof, for the house was completely surrounded by tall fir trees.

As we drew nearer the house, I smoothed down my hair and straightened my dress. I did so much want to look nice for the people who had rescued Meg and me from the poorhouse. We entered the small front garden through a large wooden gate. Here and there, hens scrabbled on the sparse lawn and stony path. A beautiful, tall, weeping willow tree stood in the centre of the lawn. Beneath its trailing leaves, sheltering from the heat of the July sun, several ducks quacked nervously as we passed, cocking their heads from side to side as if to get a better view of the strangers.

Willie and Jeanie Milne were waiting for us at the door. While we were being introduced, I gave each an exploratory glance. Willie was small and wiry, with piercing blue eyes that twinkled mischievously from his weather-beaten face. As I shook hands with him I noticed he was wearing strange trousers which finished halfway up his legs. Slightly overawed by my first sight of knickerbockers, I hastily turned towards Jeanie. She too was small, but she was plump and cuddly; her ample proportions swaddled in an all-embracing blue floral pinafore. Her pink cheeks were framed with thick, grey hair combed back neatly into a roll at the nape of her neck. When my eyes met hers I was astonished at the almost childlike innocence which shone from them. More important, however, behind those wide eyes of the deepest blue, I saw understanding, tenderness and all those things I associated with mothering.

As I wiped my feet on the old sack lying outside the door, I found myself silently praying, "Please God, please let them keep me and I promise never to be naughty as long as I live." Then, satisfied God would heed my prayer, I tripped after the Milnes into the house known as Culantyre (the back of beyond). We were shown into the room to the right where tea had been prepared for us. The long table was covered with a dazzling white linen cloth, and all down the centre plates were piled high with girdle, treacle and soda scones, iced gingerbread, and sultana and cherry cake. Everything from the butter to the raspberry jam had been made on the farm. I could hardly wait to say grace.

While the adults talked politely to each other, I ate steadily. From time to time I looked up to find Willie's eyes scanning my face and, embarrassed, I would immediately lower my eyes. Meanwhile, Jeanie fussed and clucked over the table like a broody hen, her face flushed with excitement. As her freshly baked scones and cakes disappeared, she almost purred with contentment. The men from the Corporation praised her baking profusely. I too managed a small, appreciative smile. She smiled back, her lovely eyes radiating such warmth that I blushed at this unaccustomed show of tenderness. When we had all eaten our fill, Willie escorted the Children's Officers to the main road while Jeanie showed us over our new home.

The house was sited on a small hill in the centre of the land. To the front, and far away in the distance, lay a tree-lined river which formed one boundary, whilst to the back lay swampy ground, grazing land, and another river. Between the rivers, as far as the eye could see, lay the lands of Culantyre, made up of bogs and heather, grasslands and woods and, farthest from the house where the rivers met, the arable land on which corn, hay, turnips and potatoes were grown. The house and its outbuildings formed an L shape. To the right of the house lay the milk shed, stable, byre and pigeon shed. At right angles to the pigeon shed lay the hen house, barn and a large shed that housed an assortment of carts, gigs and farm implements. In front of the stable and the byre was a deep rectangular pit surrounded by a stone causeway. This was the 'midden'. At first I found the smell of the manure somewhat overpowering, but as the days passed I not only became used to it, I rather liked it.

Culantyre boasted four rooms - two up and two down, plus a scullery. The room in which we had just had our tea was rarely used. It was in the room opposite, which served as a kitchen-cum-living room, that we spent most of our time while Jeanie laboured in the long dark scullery that led off it.

The furniture was simple, old and functional. To the right of a coal-fired stove stood a large brown leather chair. This was reserved for Willie. On the other side was a bed-chair that soon became my regular seat. A large mahogany sideboard stretched along the left-hand wall and a chaise longue, covered with a beautiful bear rug, occupied most of the right-hand wall with just enough room left for the sewing machine. Directly opposite the stove stood the most important piece of furniture – a long wooden table, capable of accommodating eight or ten people at a pinch. Above the stove the wooden mantelpiece held a marble-pillared clock, a delicate china shepherd and shepherdess, a slim double-handled glass vase containing honesty and corn, (the heads of the latter covered with coloured silver paper), a small vase containing an odd assortment of pipe cleaners and a wooden holder for letters and other odd pieces of paper. Up a very narrow steep stairway leading off from the hall, were two small attic bedrooms - one for Meg and me and one for the Milnes. Between the two attic rooms stood a small wooden book-case crammed full of books, all of which I had read before I left Culantyre.

This then was our new home. Not bristling with modern, uncomfortable furniture, nor filled with the recognised status symbols of the day, but a house glowing with warmth and a promise of love. Within these thick stone walls Meg and I were to be given as fine a home as one could ever hope for. Here all dreams were possible and all our weaknesses were added to our assets and we were the sum of the whole. In the years to come, when I found adolescence a confusing and lonely experience, like the salmon returning to the river of its birth, I would flee to Culantyre to draw strength from its hearth and to have my faith in mankind restored. And it was to Culantyre my Meg's mind wandered before, worn out by poverty and sadness, she slipped prematurely from this world. But I digress.

When Willie returned, it was time for the milking, and Meg and I stood apprehensively inside the byre as he led the cows in. First came old Daisy, a huge black and white cow with a tremendous milk capacity - no doubt due in part to the fact she was often given the calves of the other cows to foster and never did dry up. Next came Betsy, a sleek black cow whose milk was reckoned to be the creamiest in the district, then another black and white cow called Patsy. She was ever so gentle and became my favourite. Last came the red and white Ayrshire called Nellie. Of the four beasts, she alone was the proud possessor of horns. As she was inclined to be somewhat frisky, Meg and I treated her with the utmost respect, ensuring we kept well out of reach of those pretty, pointed horns.

When all the cows had been tied up and given an orange salt brick to lick, Jeannie began the milking. She always wore the same pinafore and dust cap for this task. (On those rare occasions when she was ill, Willie had to don this apparel before the cows would give him any milk). When the milking was over, the milk was transferred into huge shallow aluminium basins and placed in the cool milk shed, where, left undisturbed overnight, the cream floated to the top. I was astonished at the amount of milk stored in the milk shed and wondered how on earth four people could possibly consume so much. Morning, however, brought the answer. After the cream had been skimmed off several of the basins for our porridge and to make butter, the skimmed milk was fed to the hens. The unskimmed remainder was taken in lemonade bottles to Miss Milligan who lived beside the Chapel on the main road, or used to make delicious crowdie or milk puddings.

After Jeanie had finished her chores in the milk shed we returned to the kitchen where Willie introduced us to the four cats and two dogs that shared our new home. Snow-white was just that, snowy white all over. Bunty was black and slinky. Monty, the grey Persian, was all fluffy with beautiful blue eyes. The youngest, and the only male, was the tabby Tiger. Mona the black and white sheepdog was so loving and gentle, Tiger used to sleep beside her on her sheepskin rug. Nip, a wire-haired terrier, was less gentle and given to barking furiously when annoyed or whenever a thunderstorm threatened.

The Milnes' must have found our first evening with them tough going, for we were withdrawn and reluctant to talk about ourselves, spending most of our time avoiding their gaze and playing with the cats. (Years later Jeanie told me that when I arrived at Culantyre my eyes were blank and staring, and aware that we had been moved round a bit, had decided not to ask any questions but let nature thaw us out).

When darkness crept up, Jeanie busied herself preparing the paraffin lamps. I watched in childish fascination as she polished the glass funnel of the central hanging lamp and then the glass of the two table lamps. As she laboured away I wondered why she didn't have electricity like the people in town. I was, of course, too young to understand that in the country it cost a lot of money for such luxuries to be installed.

My next surprise came when I asked if I could go to the toilet. Jeanie said she would show me the way. I was puzzled when she lit a paraffin lamp and led me outside and round the side of the house into the back garden. But when she opened the door of a small timber hut half-hidden amongst the fruit trees, I was flabbergasted. Inside was a small wooden cupboard with a circular hole cut in the top, under which was a pail. Fitted on to the top of the cupboard was a box containing sawdust and a small shovel. Jeanie explained it was a 'dry' toilet and instructed me to sprinkle sawdust into the pail after using it. Should I only need a tinkle, however, I was to use the fields. When the pail was full it was emptied on top of the midden where the hens greedily gobbled up its contents as if they were a delicacy!

Round about 10 o'clock, Jeanie prepared a supper of bacon and eggs, followed by a variety of home baking. Although unaccustomed to eating at such a late hour, I devoured my food with relish. Meg on the other hand refused to eat the bacon and eggs, preferring instead the scones and jam. Poor Jeanie - how many times her wonderful food would be turned down for "something with jam". But she persevered, and after a few weeks, Meg began to eat the protein food so necessary for her growth.

After supper, Jeanie cleared the table, fetched a large zinc tub from the scullery, placed it on a chair in front of the stove and filled it with warm water. Meg and I washed in turn, then dressed in our new striped pyjamas, followed Jeanie up the narrow stairway to bed.

We were very tired and didn't talk much, preferring to lie between the heather-smelling sheets and listen to the noise of the river as it bustled and hustled down the route it had carved out through the centuries. I stretched out like a warm, well-fed cat beside Meg, and completely relaxed and at peace with myself, let sleep wash over me. Neither that night nor any following night did Meg nip me to keep me awake.

The following morning we awoke to the sound of Jeanie filling our wash-basin with warm water. After washing and quickly dressing, we picked our way carefully down the steep stairs, hanging on grimly to the chord banister. While we ate our porridge and cream, Willie sat on a small wooden stool in front of the stove toasting several slices of bread. After buttering them he placed them in the oven to keep warm and then busied himself with polishing our shoes until the black leather gleamed like a piece of newly-hewn coal. Every morning he followed the same routine. It was his way of becoming involved in our care.

Breakfast over, Jeanie shooed us out into the brilliant sunlight and off we went, legs flying as we rushed to explore the fields of heather and wild orchids, of myrtle and bog, cotton plants and ragged robins. The woods of slender birch and beech opened up their branches and let us peek at the birds they housed and the plants they sheltered. The rivers permitted us to plunge our naked feet into their swirling waters, and, as if in sympathy with our joy, the water bubbled round our toes, soothing and stimulating at the same time. When we had had enough of exploring, we retired to a large stone, known as 'The Big Rock', which stood, a silent sentinel, some two hundred yards from the house. We sat on top of this gigantic boulder and let the heavenly warmth of that July day wash away our memories of Foresthall. It was a relief to look over the land and know that no big fence hemmed us in or kept us out from anywhere. I felt as I imagined the genie must have felt when Abu freed him from his bottle. And whilst I could not float upwards, my soul did and every nerve in my body shouted to the sky and the birds, "I'm free, see I'm free."

When we returned to the house I opened up a little, but Meg was still on her guard. Willie and Jeanie were very patient with us. They didn't try to force their attentions upon us unduly, which was just as well, for Meg and I would not only have been embarrassed by any physical demonstration of love or tenderness, but would have found such attention abhorrent. Even today, apart from my family, I get slightly uncomfortable if anyone stands too close to me, male or female, and I was well into my thirties before I managed to force myself to touch people, no matter how fondly I may have regarded them.

The first tasks we learned that summer were those which would take up a considerable amount of our time on the farm – the provision of water and fuel.

All water came from underground springs. The well at the front of the house provided the water for the tubs for the four cows and two horses. It was also used to augment the rainwater collected and channelled from the corrugated aluminium roof into the rain barrel situated outside the milk shed. Drinking water came from the crystal-clear well at the rear of the house. When Willie took me to see it for the first time, I recoiled in horror when he pointed out the large black round beetles inhabiting it. My horror evaporated, however, when he assured me the beetles kept the water clean.

It was not a heavy task to fill the tubs for the cattle, as they were placed only a few yards from the well, but when the rain barrel was low we had to carry pails of water uphill to make up for the missing rainwater. At first we were not strong enough to carry two full pails so we started off using two National Dried Milk cans, but it didn't take long for us to realise the sooner we could carry the large pails the quicker we would fill the rain barrel.

Just as the water had to be brought to the house, so too did the fuel. Our stove was largely fired with logs and peat. The former we obtained from the small forests on our land and the latter we were allowed to cut on a neighbour's land. Willie and I worked together in the woods. He would select which tree to cut down. After he had felled it, I would set to work with a bushman saw and lop off all the branches, then Willie would hitch up the tree to Charlie, our elder horse, who dragged the denuded trunk to the shed.

As soon as Willie had positioned the tree on the wooden horse we would saw it into manageable logs. Within a year I was able to do this task by myself, using the double-handed saw with the heavy end away from me. I spent many a solitary hour in the large shed sawing away heroically and taking great pains to position the trunk in such a way that the logs fell freely. My first attempts at hacking the large logs, however, were rather frustrating. The axe, almost as big as I, seemed to have a mind of its own and frequently buried itself in a deep knot or missed the log altogether. Practise, however, soon made me reasonably skilful at avoiding the knots, and it was my party piece to cleave a log 18 inches in depth with one blow from the axe. Naturally all this sawing and hacking built up my physical strength and I was forever competing in trials of strength with the boys at school, who were impressed with my muscles, if not my femininity

Meanwhile, Meg, never as strong as I, was delegated to collect dry myrtle twigs and wood for kindling. Always the dreamer, she would saunter off towards the river, a sack over her back and a piece of grass dangling from her lips. Poor Meg - she would completely forget the time and I would frequently be sent to find her. As often as not, I would come across her sitting under the shade of a large tree happily singing to herself, her bag half-full of sticks and her mind full of daydreams. I hated to disturb her because she looked so contented and I remembered how unhappy she had been. I wanted her to find her own happiness, for my Meg was very vulnerable.

As the summer wore on, the raspberries had to be picked, and the corn and hay scythed. Both were enjoyable tasks, but for different reasons.

For the raspberry picking, Meg and I were sent to the triangular field where the rivers met and our land ended. At first I buried myself in the centre of the raspberry canes and filled my tummy before attempting to fill my baskets, but I soon learned to reverse this procedure, much to Jeanie's relief.

Each night we sorted through the berries, removing stalks and leaves which had managed to slip through our fingers. As we picked about 40 lbs. of berries each day, this was a mammoth task. Even then our work was not completed. Once the raspberries had been weighed and put into fresh baskets, Meg and I had to carry them for two miles over the bogs and along the main road to the former Manse, which was now run as a guesthouse. I enjoyed my jaunts to the Manse, not least because the two ladies who ran the guesthouse sometimes asked us to join the guests in the lounge for tea. Those raspberries that were not sold were turned into jam, and for days on end the house was full of the sweet aroma of warm raspberries, burning logs and peat. No sooner had the raspberry season finished than it was the turn of the blackberries, gooseberries, red currants, apples, pears and plums from the small rear orchard to be made into jam or puddings.

One of my fondest memories of Jeanie is of watching her stooped over a huge black pot stirring up a new batch of jam, her face flushed with the heat and her grey hair trailing down her plump cheeks. All of us, and that included the dogs, remained very quiet during those hectic nights lest we distract her from her labour of love. For, if satisfied she had made a good batch of jam, she would round off the evening by baking pancakes and girdle scones for supper - a delicious accompaniment to the newly made jams.

The other large job, that of gathering in and stacking the hay and corn, was much more onerous. After Willie had scythed the crops into long neat rows, we descended on the stubble kitted out in thick-soled boots and collected the corn and hay into bundles called stooks, which were then stacked in small groups called rooks. These were left to dry before being built into hay or corn stacks.

The building of the stacks was backbreaking work, but it gave us an opportunity to meet other people. On a given day, friends and relations would mysteriously materialise from neighbouring crofts. Together, we worked frantically all day, and sometimes by moonlight, to build the stacks and cover them with tarpaulin before the rains came. Jeanie spent most of the harvest time making sandwiches and baking scones, which she ferried back and forth throughout the day to feed the workers. If we didn't have enough cups, we used jam jars.

During our tea breaks, Meg and I discreetly eavesdropped on the adult conversations as our temporary workers regaled Willie and Jeanie with the alleged misdemeanours of neighbours and acquaintances since the last harvest.

All was not work that summer, however. Play took up the major part of the holidays. After our chores were finished, Meg and I would separate and make for our own hallowed spots. As water was an endless source of fascination for me, mine was a small island in the river to the rear of the house. Here I would sit in the shade of the young rowan trees and let my fancy roam.

Beneath the gently flowing water which brushed against 'my island', I watched rainbow trout cleave their way through their watery environs. Up stream I watched a waterfall pounding over a rocky ledge and, as the water splashed up, a myriad of rainbows encapsulated in the large drops would form a larger rainbow. Downstream there would be delicate dragonflies hovering on transparent wings over a shallow pool, and in the spring, in even more shallow pools, thousands of tadpoles would eat their way out of their sticky cells to emerge into the crystal-clear water. After they had metamorphosed into tiny green frogs, they would scatter over the land in a desperate search for food and survival.

Apart from the never-ending flow of water, the river's hold on me also lay in the wild red currant bushes lining its banks, which, in the late summer, were heavily laden with red, juicy orbs. Oh, the gluttony and the enjoyment of satisfying one's appetite in splendid isolation.

On my travels, I sometimes came across weird sights. One day I spotted what appeared to be a thick cloud floating some twenty inches above a flat stone. I ran to investigate this strange phenomenon, but curiosity turned to horror when close inspection revealed the cloud was a thick mass of flying ants. Needless to say, I didn't stay long enough to find out what they were up to in case they suddenly swooped and enveloped me in a net of crusty, nipping bodies.

Apart from all these new and wonderful experiences, that first summer at Culantyre brought two new people into our lives – Hugh and Roy Robertson. They had been evacuated to Culantyre during the war and returned every year for a holiday. Hugh was a quiet, placid type with a gentle, even temperament. Roy, the younger of the two, was much more rascally and mischievous. He had a sharp wit and a keen eye for the ludicrous, and it was not long before I found myself the butt of his humour.

In accordance with Jeanie's instructions, it was my habit to do a tinkle in the fields. One night, however, instead of making for the fields I simply headed for the comparative privacy of the old willow tree in front of the house. I had just exposed my rear when the moon, previously hidden behind a cloud, suddenly appeared, illuminating all the land and, alas, me. Immediately the sound of the violin under Roy's sensitive hands floated through the warm, moonlit air – the tune – The Pale Moon was Rising. I nearly died of shame. I felt sure he wasn't referring to the yellow summer moon, but my exposed rear quarters. When I entered the kitchen, the room was in an uproar. Even Jeanie had difficulty hiding her merriment as she pedalled away furiously on her old sewing machine.

Before that idyllic summer was over we had our first clash with Nellie, the horned Ayrshire. Meg had always been afraid of her, but on this particular morning, in order to impress the Robertsons, she had plucked up enough courage to stroke Nellie on the head. Convinced she had mastered her fear of the cow, she then skipped off towards the Big Rock with me in tow.

We had been playing for about five minutes when we heard a strange sniffling coming from the other side of the rock. Curious, we tiptoed towards the noise and came face to face with Nellie, whose small horns now seemed gigantic. Meg let out a loud yell and shot off at breakneck speed round the rock, and I, not wishing to be left, followed, but Nellie came too. Round and round we ran until Meg in a desperate attempt to escape, dashed towards the house screaming in terror. I followed, voiceless but equally terror stricken. Nellie, excited by all the commotion, pranced behind me, her horns perilously close to my backside, while Mona the sheepdog, thoroughly enjoying herself, snapped at Nellie`s hind legs. When we reached the safety of the house we hurriedly climbed over the garden gate and collapsed in an undignified heap on the other side.

Much to our chagrin, Hugh, Roy and Jeanie were waiting for us, doubled up with laughter. But by the time we managed to calm Jeanie down, for she was breathless and pained with laughing, we too saw the funny side of it. Willie later explained that having enjoyed Meg's earlier attentions, Nellie had merely been seeking more fondling. Meg, however, was never convinced of this. From that day on she kept well clear of Nellie. Each evening, when we fetched the cows home, she would hide behind a tree until I had rounded up Nellie, only re-appearing when Nellie was well past her and on her way to the byre.

One of the nicest things about the Robertsons stay with us was the endless supply of fresh fish that they provided. Although our rivers teemed with large beautiful trout, Willie never found time to go fishing. As a result, Culantyre's

5. A young Jeanie in reflective mood.

fishing season was limited to the two weeks the boys spent with us. As soon as they brought their catch home, Jeanie cooked it and served it up with skirlie, that is, oatmeal and onions fried in butter. Acutely conscious of the presence of two teenagers of the opposite sex, Meg ate her fish delicately and slowly. Unhampered by thoughts of refinement or femininity, I wolfed down the skirlie and trout as quickly as I could and presented my plate for more with an almost indecent display of gluttony.

When the supper table was cleared, Willie would stoke up the fire and we would settle round the flickering red glow to listen to Roy, an adept raconteur, while away the remaining hours of the long day with numerous tales of Edinburgh and his school.

I was entranced with his stories and the extensive vocabulary he used. As he drew towards the end of his more outrageous tales, however, I often found my eyes wandering to the still figure of Jeanie sitting on the edge of the sofa, her hands folded gracefully in front of her and her childlike blue eyes riveted on Roy. Her eyes, full of disbelief, would grow wider and wider with each word until her whole face lit up with an unbelievable innocence, and when Roy's tale was finished, she would blush like a schoolgirl before bursting into body-shaking infectious laughter. Jeanie's innocence never failed to amaze and delight me. Even now I find myself bemused at how pure and uncomplicated she was. I think her innocence stemmed from her innate goodness and tolerance. She was absolutely incapable of doing an evil act and very reluctant to attribute evil to others.

On those evenings when Roy was not entertaining us with his storytelling, he would pick up Willie's violin and play well-known Scottish tunes. Sometimes, at Willie's invitation, I would don my black pom poms and give a good imitation of the Highland Fling, my body and feet hypnotised by the music.

The two weeks Hugh and Roy spent with us passed all too quickly, but any sadness I felt at their departure was ameliorated by the knowledge that they would return to Culantyre the following year.

Not long after the boys had disappeared back to Edinburgh, a large cardboard box was left at the main road for collection. It was our year's supply of clothing from Glasgow Corporation. All our needs had been catered for – coats, winter dresses, summer dresses, gym slips, blouses, jerseys, cardigans, underwear, nightwear, footwear and even beautiful patterned handkerchiefs. We spent all evening trying on our new finery, and not until Jeanie was satisfied each garment fitted, were they all packed back into the box. I was puzzled as to how the Corporation had managed to supply us with clothes which fitted so perfectly until Meg reminded me they had taken our measurements before kitting us out for our journey to Culantyre.

The arrival of our clothing heralded the approach of the new school year. When she learned that some twenty children between the ages of four and fourteen were taught in one classroom by one teacher, Meg was cynical about the quality of education we would receive. For my part, I hoped that I would get sufficient instruction to keep me busy. I had an enquiring and competitive mind and the classroom had always been a place where those attributes had been put to full use. The outlook was not so promising for Meg. Apparently at that time it wasn't compulsory for children over the age of eleven to attend secondary school. Therefore, despite having been one of the youngest pupils to attend Mar College in Troon, she was doomed to a non-academic education.

Willie accompanied us on our first day to school. We walked through the heather and over the wood suspension bridge separating our land from that of our neighbour, a mile to the stile at the main road and then another mile until we eventually arrived at Boleskine Public School. The school building stood, solid and broody, overlooking a vast desolate moor. There were two playgrounds – one for the boys and one for the girls. But, as I later found out, most of the playing took place in the adjoining fields where the boys and girls mixed freely.

When we entered the classroom, I felt awkward and embarrassed as twenty pairs of eyes scanned Meg, Willie and me. I was even more embarrassed when I made eight errors in my first spelling test (largely due to the fact that I couldn't understand the teacher's accent).

If I had any illusions that my schooling here would be inferior, these were soon put to flight. Under the ever-alert gaze of the marvellous Miss Nicholson, I was put through my paces at a rate I have never experienced since, and it came thick and fast. What she could not cover in the classroom she more than made up for with the homework she piled on – and it worked. Her instruction was not limited to particular or general analysis, learning by rote multiplication tables or subtracting and dividing. Oh no, her teaching covered a very wide canvas.

Boys, as well as girls, were introduced to embroidery, sewing, knitting, weaving, designing wallpaper and learning old Scottish songs. When we were not occupied with these tasks, she would put us to work in her garden and at weekends she would take the older children for long rambles over miles of rough moor, all the while filling their heads with exciting snippets of Scottish history.

When she realised I loved reading she would set special tasks for me, particularly in the field of poetry. But at the age of eight or nine, poetry, unless humorous, held no fascination for me, and I was quite put out when my first school prize was a book of Robert Louis Stevenson's poems. In fact, I was well into my twenties before I found the threads and emotions she had so earnestly urged me to trace.

At our morning break we were given a mug of steaming hot National Dried Milk which, according to everyone, tasted like wall paste – which left me wondering under what circumstances they had actually tasted wall paste. Lunch consisted of two sandwiches filled with cheese or cold meat plus a cup of hot cocoa. As we all brought home-baked goodies with us, we managed to ring the changes by swapping delicacies with each other.

At four o'clock, school over for the day, Meg and I retraced our steps home, familiarising ourselves with the bogs and woods through which we passed. When we arrived back at Culantyre the table was set for dinner. I had a tremendous appetite and greedily demolished everything put in front of me, working it off later doing my chores or running endlessly from one end of the farm to the other, pretending I was guarding the homeland from the Germans. Jeanie had been cook to a very wealthy family in Mexico and enjoyed seeing me 'doing her cooking proud'. But even she was amazed at what I could eat. Each night I tucked into two platefuls of broth with potatoes, two helpings of the second course and two helpings of dessert. When you realise I probably consumed a quarter stone, i.e. three and a half pounds, of potatoes at each meal, you can understand why my appetite amazed Jeanie.

After dinner we fetched the cows home from the stubble in the far fields and attended to the water barrel and tubs before sitting down to work our way through the problems set by Miss Nicholson. Only when homework was finished and understood, did we go out to play.

As the summer melted away, autumn came bustling in and brought a new series of tasks to learn. Potatoes had to be lifted from the dry, brown earth, carted home and placed in shallow pits before being covered with dry bracken and earth to keep them safe from the rain and frost. Peats were cut and laid out to dry and sack upon sack of myrtle twigs collected before the rain rendered them useless for kindling. Hips and rowans were plucked from bushes and trees. The hips were combined with apples and made into a sweet, syrup-like jelly – truly a food for the Gods. The rowans were made into rodden jelly to be served up whenever we had venison.

Autumn was the time for settling in; a time to gather the fruits of summer and lay them by for the bleak months ahead. But for me, autumn was also a time for standing still and listening; a time to stand motionless beneath the red and yellow autumn leaves and marvel at the sheer beauty of the trees; a time to listen to the birds as they too prepared for the winter. Sometimes, when I found myself beneath the delicate yellow leaves of the birch bathed in a golden light, my body would swell with contentment, my muscles tighten and harden and as I stretched on tiptoe to touch the leaves shimmering above me, I would feel indestructible. Was I not safe here? Was I not as strong as an ox and doing well at school? The leaves above me seemed to whisper "yes" and rustle sympathetically, as if attempting to caress me, and satiated with self-adoration, I would leave my whispering trees and skip home full of hope for my future.

When the dry leaves began to forsake the trees, it was time to wrap ourselves in layer upon layer of warm clothing. We would leave for school cocooned in vests, liberty bodices, combinations, blouses, gym slips, cardigans, nap coats, woollen gloves, woollen pixies and scarves. Sandals were replaced with heavy black boots or wellingtons, inside which we wore felt slippers. All this because Jeanie had a fear of our catching pneumonia, rheumatics or the dreaded and mysterious piles! Of all our winter coverings I detested combinations most of all, and as soon as I was out of Jeanie's line of vision, I would take them off and hide them among the bracken, only donning them on my way home from school.

Between autumn and winter we celebrated Halloween. Unfortunately, because of the distances involved this was strictly a home affair – no guising. Nonetheless, we celebrated it in good style. Willie bought monstrous apples from the van which came round every Friday, and we 'dooked' for them in front of the fire. Treacle-covered scones were strung across the kitchen and we had to eat a whole one without using our hands before being allowed turns at scooping spoonfuls of whipped cream from a large bowl in which Jeanie had hidden an assortment of buttons wrapped in greaseproof paper. A large shirt button was worth a penny, a small shirt button threepence and the elusive tiny mother of pearl button, sixpence.

With the onset of the shorter days, the ground beneath our feet hardened and grew slippery. The bogs filled up with thick black ice and we spent endless hours sliding up and down them pretending to be Sonia Henie. Occasionally, we spotted a dead frog or toad spread out beneath the ice like a specimen ready for dissection and wondered why it didn't have the sense to desert the bogs before they froze over. As well as the ice, the cold weather brought the snows, and the land was covered with this glittering plaything, which provided us with material for snow fights, sledging, and most adventurous of all, igloo building.

At night, when the sky was clear and the moon shone like a beacon, I would slip outside to gaze in awe at the stars twinkling above the pristine snow dazzling beneath my feet. There, enveloped in silence, I felt very humble at my insignificance compared to the timeless snow-covered hills around me. I also thought of the tracks I had made in the snow at Monkton and of how unhappy I had been when my friends had left me. And in defiance of that awful day, I would run over the glistening, crisp surface stretching before me and experience a secret pleasure, a secret power, as I gazed at the deep footprints I left behind me. Life was just so wonderful. Then, my face flushed with the cold air and my private thoughts, I would run back into our warm kitchen, sit on the wooden stool and toast my feet in front of the fire. Oh, the loveliness of being part of a family and of being wanted.

If the snow brought a breathtaking beauty to Culantyre, it also brought more work. Extra logs had to be sawn and hacked, the cows fed with straw and the horses with hay. The sheep that we wintered also needed extra food, so the turnips stored in the unused pigeon shed were sliced up in an odd-looking machine before being scattered over the moor. At this time of the year we fed the hens a warm mash consisting of boiled potatoes, turnips and meal. It smelt so wonderful I was often tempted to eat it myself.

About 10 o'clock in the evening, Willie, Meg and I made our way to the cold, dark barn to thresh the corn which was fed to the cows before they were locked in for the night. I hated this chore, because at 10 o'clock I was usually ensconced in front of the fire reading a book and I resented being disturbed. Once inside the barn, Willie would climb on to the seat of the threshing machine and pedal as fast as he could while I pushed the handle round. When sufficient speed had been achieved, he would feed the corn through the drum where the heads were torn off by huge teeth and deposited on the ground whilst the straw shot out to be forked away by Meg. We had two accidents while threshing. Once Meg touched the drum with her fork, the fork head broke off and shot across the barn like a missile but fortunately missed her. On another occasion, I was careless when handing up a stook to Willie and my right arm was caught in the wheel that turned the drum. Alerted by my screams, Willie immediately stopped pedalling and I escaped with a rather nasty burn mark but no broken bones. After the corn had been threshed the straw was collected into two piles – one to feed the cows and one for their bedding. The corn heads were scooped up and placed in the large chute of the bruiser for bruising on Saturday.

Bruising was a long and heavy job and because Meg was afraid of the dark and I was the stronger, this onerous task fell upon me. As there were no windows in the barn and the only light came through the door, it would take several minutes for my eyes to adjust sufficiently to the darkness to let me see to work. For some strange reason I found it easier to bruise the corn by pushing the handle of the bruiser round with my legs rather than with my arms. This I did by climbing up on a sack, bracing my back against the wall, supporting my weight with my hands, also braced against the wall, and slowly pushing the large handle round with my muscular legs. The corn was sucked through two large rollers at the bottom of the chute and pressed flat before falling into a large basin below. Later, the bruised corn was mixed with the strong black treacle that we stored in a large drum in the barn and fed to the cows and horses. As treacle for domestic consumption was rationed, Jeanie used a little from the drum to make scones, gingerbread and puddings. Willie was concerned lest 'the authorities' found out, so we were sworn to secrecy over this 'misappropriation' of treacle supplied for animal consumption only.

One of our most enjoyable winter tasks was the collection of our year's supply of coal. Out would come the great wooden sledge, which Willie would harness on to Bute, the gentle Clydesdale, before Meg and I climbed inside. It was most uncomfortable but we loved being thrown from side to side as the sledge slid over the rough track. Willie, I'm convinced, deliberately chose the roughest route just to hear our mixed squeals of fear and excitement. When we reached the road we helped hump the heavy sacks into the sledge then off Bute went, panting and snorting as she hauled the coal home. Charlie, Bute's companion, was never used for heavy work because, not only was he getting on in years, he was becoming a little irascible. On one occasion after Meg had climbed on to his back, he tossed her over his head and for several minutes pranced ominously close to her prostrate body. Meg never attempted to ride again and I limited myself to riding Bute, despite the fact my legs were far too short to encompass her big body.

During the winter months, in order to give us time to get home before darkness fell, school would end an hour earlier. However, this extra hour did nothing to alleviate my fear of crossing the suspension bridge when it was covered with frost or ice. On those occasions, bravado took a holiday, and I crossed the bridge on all fours.

When the long nights forced us indoors, I spent my time either reading or building cardboard doll's houses, which I peopled with little cardboard dolls that Jeanie drew and cut out for me. Sometimes, however, we would gather round the fire and with the lamp turned low, listen to one of Jeanie's ghost stories. She had a never-ending supply of tales concerning the strange happenings that occurred long ago in mysterious, unidentified hills and woods. The most wonderful thing about her storytelling was the fact that she displayed the same wide-eyed innocence narrating them as she did when listening to Roy's somewhat embroidered tales of Edinburgh. As she regaled us with legends passed down from generation to generation, her pupils would dilate as she amazed herself with the wonder of it all. I often found myself smiling, not at the story, but the narrator, who was more mystified by her own tales than her listeners. She never understood why I smiled half-way through her tales and, puzzled, would stop, and cock her head to the side and stare questioningly at me. Not until she was satisfied that I was listening with the required respect would she carry on.

Her favourite story concerned an elderly spinster who allegedly once lived beside a 'bottomless' loch on the land adjoining Culantyre. The spinster was reputed to be very wealthy and one day two strangers turned up at her croft. After accepting her hospitality, they tied her up and demanded to know where she kept her money. The old lady refused to talk, so they put her down her well, covered it and left her to 'stew' for an hour, hoping that when they returned she would reveal where she had hidden her money. Unfortunately, when they returned, not one but several hours later, the spinster was dead. A few weeks later one of the robbers, overcome with remorse, confessed his crime to the police and when the old lady was removed from her "blood-red"` watery grave they found "thousands of pounds" sewn into her thick plaited hair. According to Jeanie, this particular well turned blood red on each anniversary of the spinster's death. About two years after hearing this story, I visited the well where the poor old lady was said to have died. The water was indeed red, but it was rust-red from the decaying corrugated iron that had slipped into the well. I never did have the heart to disillusion Jeanie, so when I told her I had seen this strange phenomenon, I gave her a lurid description of the red, red water.

As our first Christmas at Culantyre approached, Jeanie busied herself over the old sewing machine, painstakingly making kilts and satin blouses for our first school party. (She had obtained the silk from rescued parachutes). The party was held in a hall about five miles from Culantyre, a location chosen because it was centrally situated in relation to the other small schools with whom we would be sharing it. I was fair tingling with self-importance when I entered the hall dressed in my first kilt. My ego took a massive dent, however, when I found that about 80% of the children had turned up in similar attire.

This was an occasion for extroverts, and never slow to push myself forward, I was first in line to take the stage. I put my heart and soul into a dramatic rendering of a poem about a shark and a flying fish – quite a feat considering I really didn't understand the poem. Meg, however, could not be enticed on to the stage and spent most of the evening hiding from Miss Nicholson's searching eyes.

Culantyre's isolated situation may have been idyllic, but when it came to the choosing and buying of Christmas gifts, it presented Meg and me with several problems. Firstly, we had to choose our presents from a catalogue, fill in the form and secretly hand it and our money to Maggie, the postwoman, to post for us. Secondly, when the goods arrived we had to be warned. This Maggie did by leaving two stones on top of our post box (which was about a mile from the farm). The following day she would deliver the parcels, which we collected and hid in our bedroom for distribution on Christmas Eve.

That first Christmas, Meg delegated me to leave the Milnes' presents downstairs. About two in the morning, I tiptoed stealthily from the bedroom, a dimly lit paraffin lamp in one hand and the presents clutched to my chest with the other. Unfortunately, I was unaware that Mona, the sheepdog, sometimes slept on the stairway. Consequently, as I slowly lowered my right leg on to the third step down I was surprised to find it was soft and warm. Before I could digest this piece of sensory information, Mona yelped and hurriedly scrambled to her feet. I fell over her and bounced down the narrow stairway, holding on like grim death to the paraffin lamp and scattering my parcels around me like a drunken, airborne Santa.

Luckily, the lamp went out on the first jolt, and, although drenched in paraffin, I wasn't set alight. For a few moments I struggled blind and bewildered in the folds of the heavy velvet curtain at the foot of the stairs. When I finally managed to extricate myself, I saw Jeanie silhouetted against the kitchen door, her eyes wide and staring as she tried to make sense of what had happened. Alarmed in case she picked up one of the rifles kept in the hall, I cried out in terror. "It's only me. It's only me, Mrs. Milne." Explanations over, I placed the presents on the table, changed into a clean pair of pyjamas then crept silently back upstairs while Mona fixed me with a mournful, accusing stare.

In the morning we awoke to find our stockings filled with presents, among which was a parcel containing a long letter from father. It was the first communication we had received from him since leaving Glasgow. Glasgow Corporation, through whom all correspondence had to be channelled, had heavily censored the letter. All place names and the names of people had been inked out. He had changed digs and started a new job as a furniture remover. There was no mention of mother and no word about our future. Despite those omissions we had a wonderful Christmas.

As the days began to lengthen, daring snowdrops and crocuses poked their green shoots through the cold earth. Eventually the last snow melted, the swollen mountain streams poured down the hills and the dried out bogs filled, saturating the dehydrated mosses until they became plump and resilient underfoot, like a plush, red and green carpet. Spring had arrived and with it came the lambing season.

Day after day Willie and Mona ranged over the hills and moors looking for sheep or lambs in trouble. When a sheep lost a lamb he would take another from a mother who had twins. After covering it with the skin of the dead lamb, he would present it to the stricken mother, who, fooled by the smell, would accept the lamb as her own. Sometimes, when it was the mother who had died, he would bring the orphan lamb home to be nursed.

One spring, as I was walking to school through our neighbour's land, the piteous bleating of a young lamb caught my attention. When I approached, its frightened mother ran off and stood guard some twenty yards away. The lamb repeatedly tried to struggle to its feet, but it was too weak to stand. I had to do something. I hurriedly picked several handfuls of grass, hand-fed some to the lamb, left the rest within her reach, and before continuing my journey to school, gave her water to drink from the little bottle I carried for cleaning my slate. When I returned from school the lamb was still lying in the same place. I plucked more grass for her and gave her another bottle of water while her mother watched from some distance away.

As we had strict instructions not to meddle with animals belonging to other farmers, I didn't tell Jeanie about the lamb. The following morning I secretly filled my small water bottle with milk – the guilt I felt at this deception was more than compensated for by the nuzzling, guzzling appreciation of my poor lamb. For two weeks I kept up the routine of feeding her on my journeys to and from school. Day by day she grew stronger and bigger, but for her to survive she must learn to walk, and to help her achieve this I purloined an old sack from the shed and hid it in my school satchel. On my return journeys from school, I slid it under the lamb's belly, lifted her till her feet just trailed on the ground and walked her up and down. She loved it. At first she could only use her front legs but as these strengthened she began to put some weight on her emaciated hind legs. Finally the day arrived when I found her standing, albeit shakily, on all four legs and when she stumbled to meet me I cried with joy. But when she started gambolling to meet me I knew it was time to stop feeding her. Oh, how it hurt, ignoring her butting head and her beautiful liquid eyes as she searched my person for food. But I had to be strong, refuse to give in to her demands. Eventually she stopped greeting me whenever I appeared and stayed with the flock.

While the lambing season was in full swing, round in the back garden the hens were busy hatching their fluffy yellow chickens. When they were older we had to train them to go into the hen house at night. Meg and I detested this task, not because we had to grab them and stuff them unceremoniously into a sack before releasing them in the hen house, but because we could never gauge how long it would take. Sometimes it only took fifteen minutes but there were occasions when it took almost half an hour to catch a particularly wily chicken. After a week or two of this treatment, the chickens learned to make their own way to the hen house and Meg and I would heave a sigh of relief. The nightly battles were over – at least for another year.

One year, because we were inexplicably low in eggs, Jeanie had to send to the town for chickens. They arrived in ventilated cardboard boxes, but the journey had been too much for some who were dead on arrival. We segregated the weak from the strong and tried desperately to revive those showing signs of distress. One in particular was so weak Willie said it would be futile to attempt to resuscitate it, but I tried. I gently warmed it in front of the fire, caressed it and fed it drops of brandy from an eyedropper. It opened its eyes once or twice, but in a moment of carelessness, I let the little bundle of yellow fluff roll from my hands into the hot ashes beneath the stove. When I retrieved it, the chicken was dead. I was inconsolable, convinced that my carelessness had caused its death. Willie tried to convince me it had been dead before it rolled out of my hands, but I didn't believe him. He explained that in the animal kingdom it was survival of the fittest and that my little chicken had fallen at the first hurdle. But I didn't want to listen; couldn't understand why the chicken had to die and thought the laws of nature were not only stupid but also wicked.

I went through the same agonies when I lost Bunty, my favourite cat. She was old and often wandered away for days on end. When she failed to return to the farm after a particularly long absence, the Milnes tried to allay my fears by suggesting she had wandered on to another farm and decided to stay there. However, during an argument, Meg blurted out that she had found Bunty hanging dead over a branch in the river. Without waiting to find out where, I ran down to the river to the front of the house and in a state of extreme agitation searched high and low for her. Eventually I spotted her, at least what remained of her, draped over a branch lying just inches above the water. I was strangely quiet for almost a month, and as further proof of my sadness I even went off my food – a sure sign, said Willie, that I had truly loved my Bunty.

Fate, however, played a nasty trick on Meg, who should have known better than to inform me of the dead Bunty's whereabouts. Her favourite cat, the small tabby Tiger, met his death in a most tragic way. All our cats had been born and nursed in the byre, and it was not unusual for them to sleep on top of the cows during the cold winter nights. One night, however, Tiger strayed beneath Meg's favourite cow, Daisy, who sat on top of him and crushed him to death. Meg was very upset, particularly as poor Tiger had been flattened to almost twice his normal length.

Apart from the lambs and the chickens, spring brought our first calf – Michael. He was white all over with a grey nose and looked very fragile as he stood shaking on his long delicate legs, his large watery eyes gazing wildly around him. I was given the task of training him to drink milk from a pail. After dipping my fingers in the milk, I would present them to the curious Michael, who would suck them lovingly and long. Slowly, I would lead his mouth down to the pail, but at first he persisted in breathing the milk up his nose and snorting it out in bubbles. After a few days, however, he learned milk should be sucked in through his mouth, and I was able to reserve my fingers for more delicate tasks. When he was ready, he was lassoed and dragged reluctantly outside by Willie, who held tightly on to the rope while Michael ran round in circles until he was tired out. I never did understand the lassoing. Whether it was to prevent the calf from running itself to death or to keep it from running away, remained a mystery.

The main spring task was ploughing the fields before planting the potatoes. Charlie and Bute were used alternately for this chore. Once or twice Willie let me take over the plough, but when I discovered ploughing a straight line was not as easy as it looked, I confined my activities to helping him spread manure from the midden between the furrows.

When the potatoes were planted and the turnip, cabbage and corn seed sown, it was time to open up the potato pits in the back garden to remove the young sprouting shoots. This was a tedious and lengthy job but it was essential if the potatoes were to remain nice and firm till the new crop was ready.

Our second summer brought Willie's nieces and nephews to the farm for a holiday. Iain, Jimmy and Nana Morrison came every year after that, occupying the rarely used room to the right of the hall. Those were blissful days when our house was filled with noise and laughter, days remembered as being spent playing in perpetual sunlight, although I know it must have rained occasionally.

I think it was our third summer when Cathy arrived. She had been evacuated to the Milnes but had returned voluntarily to stay at Culantyre until she left school.

And so the seasons came and went, one year following another. Meg, my frail Meg, blossomed into a beautiful woman with rosy cheeks and milk-white skin. When she reached fifteen she was employed as a maid in the Manse guesthouse but this didn't last too long. The lure of the town was too much for her, and one day she packed her bags, hitched a lift in a coal lorry and made for Inverness, where she got a job as a Nanny to a very respectable family.

Left on our own, Cathy and I grew very close. She was very pretty with shoulder-length curly auburn hair, a slim figure and monstrous blue eyes, which sparkled with a "je ne sais quoi". I had straight short hair, a muscular body and, so I was told, probing eyes. In short, we were Beauty and the Beast. When my breasts began to grow, my lack of confidence in my appearance escalated. I found this sign of approaching maturity very embarrassing, particularly as I was the most well-developed girl in the school. As my figure changed, so too did my behaviour. No longer could I be found walking on my hands, my strong thighs waggling in the air and my navy flannel knickers on view to all. Great care was taken to sit 'ladylike' to prevent anyone seeing above my knees, and formerly enjoyable games with the boys became less boisterous.

I needn't have worried. As far as the boys were concerned, I was just like one of them. No allowance was ever made for my femininity – after all, could I not wield a shinty stick like one of them; kick a ball as far as any boy and, most damning of all, humiliate them by becoming the school-wrestling champion! Whether their apparent disinterest in me was entirely due to my physical prowess or the fact that it was no secret Jeanie kept tabs on my journeys to and from school, I don't know, but I suspect the local boys found my well-advertised strength not only challenging, but intimidating. Catherine on the other hand was considered to be the epitome of femininity, and despite Jeanie's telescope, the boys vied with each other for the privilege of carrying her school satchel. When she left Boleskine School to attend the secondary school in Foyers, the boys practically ignored me.

In the spring of 1949 I sat the mandatory eleven plus and, like everyone else, had to wait weeks for the result. Sometime in late May or early June, Miss Nicholson told me to tell Willie she wanted to see him. I broke out in a sweat. Was she going to tell him about my rudeness the previous week. This incident centred round a foster child who lived on a nearby farm. Her foster parents had asked Miss Nicholson to strap her because her hands were 'dirty'. This thin, nervous creature had come to me and shown me her hands, which were covered in chaps, that is to say, weals that form when wet skin is exposed to cold air. Not unnaturally, she was reluctant to scrub them. I couldn't bear this injustice. I knew the little girl worked for long hours outside on the farm, and when she was called out to take her punishment, I protested. I even went so far as to suggest it was her foster parents who should be strapped for allowing her hands to become so painful. This confrontation was resolved by a judgement that might have come straight from Solomon himself! I was strapped instead.

Now, as I trudged home with Miss Nicholson's summons, I was fearful of the consequences of my outburst, for although life at Culantyre was very pleasant, it was so because everyone knew the rules and worked within them. By no stretch of the imagination would rudeness to a teacher be considered acceptable behaviour. As soon as I arrived home, I passed on Miss Nicholson's request to Willie.

I was washing myself in the zinc tub when he returned. He looked very stern. My whole body twisted into a knot as I waited for his anger to explode. Instead, he settled into his armchair, took a pipe from the pipe rack, lit it and puffed away for a few minutes before quietly asking, "What sort of composition did you write for the Bursary, Jound?" My heart jumped into my mouth and sweet sensations ran up and down my spine. I had passed. I had passed. Willie repeated his question. I replied that I had written about a stray Alsatian dog rescuing a boy from a frozen pond. To my amazement and delight, he told me Miss Nicholson had received a request from "people from the Education Department" to see samples of my previous essays. Apparently, despite the fact the exam had been supervised by Peggy the Manse, they were making sure that I, not Miss Nicholson, had written the essay. (In adulthood I find this story sounds preposterous, and yet I have it firmly etched in my mind.) I had won essay competitions set by the RSPCA and Meg had won similar competitions set by other societies, but to have experienced examiners think my work was that of an adult, was praise indeed.

That night, I bathed in the warm pride of the Milnes. I couldn't have given them a better present. Fully aware of my dreams and aspirations, they had done everything possible to build my self-confidence and now I would have the opportunity to test and stretch my mind at Inverness Academy. When I retired to bed, I fell asleep convinced I had a guardian angel looking after me. The following morning I wrote to father telling him my good news.

July came and went without a word from Glasgow Corporation. By mid-August we began to think the unthinkable – they couldn't find another foster home for me. Exasperated, Willie voiced his frustration at the Corporation. "Why can't they just place you in the hostel used by the other girls from the Highlands and Islands who attend the Academy? Too damn simple for them." I agreed. I had secretly nourished the hope I might be sent to the hostel – not because I didn't want to be re-fostered, but because I thought it would be nice to live with girls of my own age who shared my interests. Now I was more concerned that if no foster home could be found for me I wouldn't be given the chance to learn Latin, French, Science or Maths.

Willie and I were in the pigeon shed when Jeanie rushed in waving a telegram from the Corporation. It read, "Have Helen ready for removal on Thursday." The large veins in Willie's temples bulged and zigzagged as he exploded with anger. "You'd think she was a piece of furniture," he shouted. Never too fond of officials at any time, this was the last straw. He had always resented visiting officials taking the lids off the pans on our stove to see what was inside, particularly as there were fostered children not far from Culantyre whose harsh living conditions were apparent to everyone except the visiting officials. I loved this aggressive side of Willie. No one could intimidate him. I suspect I owe a little of my personality to his influence. Before leaving Culantyre, encouraged by his openly expressed dislike of the Corporation, I plucked up the courage to tell him about my confrontation with Miss Nicholson over the little girl with the chapped hands. When I finished talking, he just smiled, winked at me and said, "Aye, Jound, you're fit for any of them, but don't tell Jeanie. She won't understand."

I spent my last days at Culantyre visiting all my old haunts, quietly thanking them for the joys they had given me – the Big Rock round which Nellie had chased Meg and me and on whose summit I had fondly sat imagining I ruled the world; the rivers where I had watched the trout play and the water dance, and lastly, my secret island where I sat under the rowan trees now heavy and drooping with berries, and thought solemn thoughts. There, as the sun made endless, moving patterns on the flat rocks, I closed my eyes, listened to the gentle gurgling noises of the water, smelt the growing greenness around me and wept. I wept for all those children who would never see the lovely things I had seen and who would never escape from poverty because they had been crushed before they had fully grown. I was lucky. I was a survivor.

During the following days, while I flitted in a trance from one favourite spot to another, Jeanie was caught up in a whirlpool of preparations – preparations for my departure and preparations for the arrival of two girls she had been persuaded to take in my place. When Thursday arrived I was far too excited to be of any use to anyone, so Jeanie sent me outside to keep a look out for the newcomers while she prepared the front room for their arrival.

It was early afternoon when I spotted them through the telescope - two adults and three children. I looked again. There were definitely three children. Jeanie and Willie both peered through the glass. There was no doubt about it. The Corporation was bringing three children to replace me. If Willie and Jeanie were annoyed, they kept their annoyance to themselves.

When the girls and their escorts arrived, they were ushered into the rarely used front room for tea. During the meal, when I stretched out my arm in front of one of the newcomers, she flinched and tilted her body backward in an avoiding movement. I looked up at Willie and Jeanie. Our eyes conveyed our unspoken thoughts. Another bruised and frightened child had been placed in their care. I smiled inwardly. Jeanie who had cared for me would now do the same for the three children at her table. They had nothing to fear. Here they would be safe.

After tea, it was time to say goodbye. Jeanie handed me a large brown paper bag full of home baking. I shook hands with her, Willie and Cathy, then I followed my escorts past the same ducks I had encountered on my arrival at Culantyre four years previously.

6. Left to right - Jeanie with her brothers Alex and Duncan.

6

CHAPTER SIX
Crossroads

As no one spoke to me on the journey to Inverness, I whiled away the time fantasising about my new foster home, the Academy and the pleasures living in a town could provide. Sometimes, however, my daydreaming was interrupted by an unwelcome observation. The lady sitting beside the chauffeur bore a remarkable resemblance to the woman who had taken me to Foresthall. I hadn't noticed it at Culantyre. Now, forced to stare at the back of her head, I was sure I saw a similarity.

But I was too excited to let this niggling thought spoil my daydreaming for long.

When the car finally stopped in front of a wooden gate leading to what I think was a council house, a thin lady rushed down the pathway, leaned defensively over the gate and shouted "I'm sorry, I can't take her. My cousin is coming to stay." My escort left the car to remonstrate with the thin lady, but she wouldn't budge, either from her decision or the gate. After what seemed an eternity, they separated. The thin lady ran back to the sanctuary of her house and my escort climbed back into the car. "Well, I never," she exploded, "Fancy leaving it as late as this to tell us." The chauffeur grunted. I was devastated. I would have to go back to Culantyre and attend the local Junior Secondary at Foyers. Now I would never get my Highers. Then I realised I couldn't go back to Culantyre – there was no room. There were now three children in my place. Perhaps after all I would be placed in the hostel.

I was mulling over this possibility when my escort turned to the chauffeur. "Well, we'll have to find somewhere to leave her." Time stood still. I was now convinced she was the person who had taken me to Foresthall. I had hated that lady then and I hated this woman now. Nothing had changed. I still had no control over my destiny.

As I was touted around Inverness, I went through the same gamut of emotions I had experienced when I had trailed round Glasgow with Dad and Meg at the end of the war. But there was a subtle difference. I felt resentful at the cavalier way in which my future was being handled by those paid to supervise it. Did they think I belonged to a subhuman species; was blind, deaf and without feelings? I decided the best policy was to display no emotion whatsoever, so I sat with my back straight, my head erect and my hands folded in my lap as the plump lady frantically tried to find me an alternative foster home. Naturally, no one was prepared to take me in at such short notice. In fact, upon hearing I was to attend the Academy, one homely-looking lady rejected me on the grounds that I would be too clever to fit into her household. "How can you be too clever?" I asked myself.

As the afternoon dragged on, my escort became more and more agitated. She finally decided to try a house directly opposite the Academy where three other children had already been placed. This time we were invited into the front parlour. I have a vague memory of thick velvet curtains and velvet upholstered chairs. The three elderly Cameron sisters, Christine, Maggie and Peggy, listened politely as my predicament was explained. They decided that they couldn't agree to take me in without consulting their brother Robert, who wasn't due home for another half-hour. My escort had no option but to wait for Robert's return. While she waited in the front parlour, Peggy, the youngest of the sisters, beckoned me to follow her into the back room.

There was only one word for that room – Dickensian. One wall was lined with ceiling-high dark green wooden cupboards; the opposite housed a large coal-fired range. Next to the wall facing the window were two wooden benches and a long table. Peggy introduced me to the three children who were sitting round the table – Nigel, a coloured eleven-year-old with a lively face and mischievous laughing eyes, Marie a girl of about eight and another boy of about twelve, whose name completely escapes me. When Peggy left us alone a long silence ensued before Nigel started to fire questions at me in quick succession. When he had satisfied his curiosity, he shrugged his shoulders and said, "It's not bad here if you do as you're told. Noise that's what upsets them, noise," and he winked all-knowingly at me.

About half an hour later, feverish activity and inaudible whispers in the hallway heralded the arrival of Robert. He popped his head round the door, looked me over and grunted before disappearing up the hall and into the parlour. That initial brief sighting of Robert Cameron sent shivers up and down my spine. He looked dour and sullen. I knew instinctively that he was a strict disciplinarian, and when Peggy re-appeared to tell me I would be staying with them, my heart sank. Of my plump escort there was no sign.

At Peggy's invitation, Nigel led me upstairs to my bedroom. I was pleasantly surprised. It was bright and airy with a large double bed. As Nigel looked on, I unpacked my case and hung my clothes in a large wardrobe, which was already half full of clothes. When I asked to whom the clothes belonged, he replied that they were Maggie's. "Why doesn't she keep them in her own room?" I asked. Nigel laughed. "This is her room," he replied. "You'll be sharing it and the bed with Maggie and Marie."

When we returned to the room-cum-kitchen, the table was set for four. "Where do the adults eat?" I enquired. Irritated by my 'stupidity', Nigel sighed, "They eat in their own room silly, except on Sundays." My surprise at being segregated from the adults was offset by my relief at learning I wouldn't need to sit opposite the dour Robert during meals. My first evening meal at the Camerons consisted of porridge followed by bread and jam and as the days passed I learned that porridge, bread and jam were served for tea Monday to Friday without exception. Later that evening, as I helped Nigel wash up the tea dishes in the scullery adjoining the kitchen, I observed that the Camerons preferred a different diet. Nigel explained this away by pointing out that whereas we had a cooked meal at school, the Camerons had theirs in the evening. Further conversation with Nigel left me in no doubt that in this household the less children were seen or heard the better. The Camerons it seemed, lived a totally separate life from the children, except on Sundays, when they joined us for a cooked breakfast in the kitchen and we were invited in the evening for tea and cake in their sitting room, which was across from the front parlour.

About eight o'clock, whilst it was still light, we were shooed off to bed. Marie fell asleep almost instantaneously. However, for me, accustomed to running over the moors till ten in the evening, sleep was impossible. When Maggie joined us about 9 p.m., she fell asleep within minutes, but for me sleep still remained elusive. Firstly, because Maggie snored loudly and secondly, as she was well into her seventies, she reminded me painfully of the elderly women I had met in the poorhouse. It seemed that what I had considered to be a move full of promise, had turned into a nightmare. I tried to console myself with the thought that the Camerons had been taken by surprise and that this was probably only a temporary arrangement. When I subsequently realised, however, that it wasn't, I took steps to ensure my sleeping arrangements would be altered.

The following morning, after a breakfast of porridge, bread and jam, Nigel took me to the local golf course. I was puzzled when he insisted we hide in the trees at the edge of the green, but soon all was revealed. Nigel was waiting to retrieve lost balls, which he could sell later for sixpence. By the end of the morning we had nine balls between us, which we discreetly exchanged for four shillings and sixpence in the back room of a well-known sports shop in the town centre. During the remainder of my stay with the Camerons I used my share of the golf ball money to buy fish and chips to augment my porridge teas.

My first Saturday at the Camerons found me immersed in household chores about which I knew very little. At Culantyre, apart from tidying my bedroom and occasionally wiping over the linoleum in the hall with diluted milk to give it a shine, I had spent most of my time outdoors. Now, under the eagle eye of the eldest sister, Christine, I was introduced to new and numerous chores. During the week I took my turn at washing the dishes and cleaning the knives with bathbrick. On Friday evenings, as well as my own clothes, I also washed Marie's. At first I found it difficult to do the washing without making a terrible mess, but eventually I managed to master this task with the minimum of effort and in the shortest time possible. On Saturday mornings I blacked the range in the kitchen, cleaned my shared bedroom, the stairway, hall, kitchen and scullery that led off it. If I finished all my tasks by eleven o'clock, I was allowed to go to the La Scala morning matinee with the rest of the children. Peggy who worked there at an unidentified part-time job gave us complimentary tickets for the matinee. I loved going to the cinema and would return in the afternoon at my own expense to lose myself, not only in the dramas, but also in the immaculate screen homes and beautiful clothes, which no one ever seemed to clean.

In the evening, after I did the ironing, Nigel and I would slip over the back garden wall into the school playground on the other side, where we spent an hour or so swinging from the metal bars supporting the roof of the bicycle shed. Nigel was most athletic and although I couldn't match his natural agility and grace, when it came to trials of brute strength, I held my own.

As at Culantyre, Sunday was a day of rest, but there the resemblance ended. Here it was a day given over to showing one's gratitude to the Lord by being very serious. Laughter on the Sabbath was considered to be a wicked thing. In the morning the Camerons joined us in the kitchen for a breakfast of bacon and eggs. Breakfast over, dressed in our Sunday best and armed with a penny for the collection and mints to suck during the sermon, we trooped *en masse* to the local church for Morning Service. After lunch, which the children ate alone, we attended Bible Class. In the evening we returned to church yet again. But this was not the end of our religious instruction. After the evening service we were treated to tea and cake in the front sitting room before Robert read a doom-prophesying passage from a huge bible. Our due respects having been paid to the Lord and Robert, we were sent to bed. So much godliness and so little humanity!

The following morning, despite another disturbed night, I was up bright and early to prepare for my first day at the Academy. After a short service in the Assembly Hall, the rector informed us, that is to say the newcomers, that we were the inheritors of a fine tradition and were expected to conduct ourselves with propriety both inside and outside the school. We were instructed that we must walk from one classroom to another in a clockwise direction at all times. Anyone caught disobeying this rule would receive a mandatory forty minutes detention. All first year students would be taught the same subjects to the same level, and, depending upon the results, would be graded the following year. Thus, from the very beginning, we were competing against each other.

I loved the competitive atmosphere. Out Latin teacher, Miss Thom, wasted no time on lengthy introductions. During our first lesson she made it quite clear that she expected us to learn our conjugations until we could recite them as easily as the ten times table. A strict disciplinarian, she combined her punishments with an obsession for raising funds for sports and school outings. Pupils were fined one penny for minor misdemeanours and each week the fine went unpaid, it was doubled. She augmented her fund raising by baking cheese biscuits, for which the pupils provided the ingredients and were charged one penny per biscuit!

When I returned home from my first day at the Academy I was full of everything that I had seen, heard and done. It was all so new and exciting. A week had barely passed when Christine told me I was a smarty pants and a proper little madam, and the sooner I realised that what I did was of no interest to anyone, the happier everyone would be. Hurt and unable to comprehend that town dwellers, unlike country folk, could find their own mental stimulation and didn't need or desire a running commentary on other people's activities, I shut up and immersed myself in my books.

As the days passed and my homework increased, I found that after my evening chores, which included supervising Marie's homework, I had little time left for studying, for there was no question of my being allowed to put the light on in the bedroom. I decided to put this right by any means I could. And so began my deception. Night after night I faked horrendous nightmares until Maggie had had enough and I was 'banished' to the box room in the attic. There was no electric light and hardly enough room in which to stand up, but it was mine, all mine. I had a hidey-hole of my own. I was supplied with a ration of candles, which I augmented with others bought with my golf ball money and the profit I made from selling kindling to neighbours. (I made the kindling from orange boxes Robert brought home from the grocery store where he worked – self-sufficiency being considered next to godliness).

New school subjects and fish suppers notwithstanding, I soon became homesick for Culantyre. I missed the unspoken love of the Milnes, Jeanie's cooking and the long conversations we had round the dinner table. I also began to appreciate how relaxing it had been to wander over the moors and play unobserved. When I asked if I could spend a weekend at Culantyre, I was sharply reminded that they, the Camerons, were now my guardians and I had to forget Culantyre.

Mild discomfort now turned to resentment. As far as I was concerned, the Milnes were my family. I now felt cut off from the people who I loved and who loved me. I wanted so much to tell them how well I was doing at school and all about the new subjects I was being taught. I couldn't see what harm could result from allowing me to visit the farm, particularly as the Camerons seemed to want me to behave passively, like a shadow. But I wasn't a shadow. I was a flesh and blood extrovert. Then fate intervened. In October a new boy came to stay. In order to give him time to settle in, it was decided I should go to Culantyre for a weekend. I needed no encouragement. I packed my school case with a selection of my textbooks and fled back to my beloved moors.

I was welcomed like the prodigal son. Over dinner, as I tucked into soup, bacon roly-poly and steamed pudding, I recounted everything that had happened to me since I had left. I was in a state of uncontrolled elation and it poured out in a hysterical stream. When I paused for breath, I waited to hear what the newcomers had to say about their day, but they remained silent. Surely they must have done something that was worth mentioning. Willie read my thoughts. He stared into my eyes, sighed and said, "Aye, Jound, things have changed. We don't hear much about what's going on in the Strath now," and he looked unusually wistful. Strange - my new foster parents couldn't stand my chattering but Willie obviously missed it.

For two whole days I entertained the Milnes with stories about my new school, the Camerons and the wily and athletic Nigel, adding a few embellishments as I went along in order to bring a little humour into my tales. From time to time Willie would interrupt me to say, "Aye, Jound, you're fit for them," and although I would smile in agreement, I knew 'fit for them' I most certainly was not.

By the end of my stay, I think Willie had seen through my front; had picked up I was not in an environment which was helping me grow. Christine's assertion that I would have to leave school at fifteen and work in a shop like everyone else had appalled him. He tried to reassure me the Corporation wouldn't let that happen and to convince me that the five years I would have to wait before going to University would soon pass. "Hang on Jound, hang on," he muttered as he poked the fire and brushed his hand across his eyes. "A spark," he said, but it was the first and last tear I ever saw in Willie Milne's eyes. He had not named me Jound (his pronunciation of the Gaelic for nettle) without just cause. He knew that my volatile and fiery nature would make it impossible for me "to hang on." The same characteristic which had made me protest about the injustice of strapping a girl because her hands were chapped would, given time, inevitably lead me to challenge my living conditions.

When I returned to the Camerons, I returned with a renewed faith in myself. I was not, after all, a smarty pants or a little madam. I was just in the wrong foster home. I also brought with me a letter asking if I could spend my Christmas holidays at Culantyre. The Camerons did not take too kindly to this request and told me that I would never be allowed to return to Culantyre. This was my home and I would fit in, like it or not. No allowance was going to be made for my affectations, and, as if to make the point, despite it being the Sabbath, I was ordered into the scullery to do the washing I had cunningly avoided by spending the weekend with the Milnes.

I was in the kitchen pounding away in the sink when Christine introduced me to the newcomer – a fourteen-year-old boy who also attended Inverness Academy. I took an instant dislike to him. My relationships with the boys at Boleskine School had been limited to tomboyish skirmishes. I now found myself on the receiving end of teenage innuendo with which I was ill-equipped to cope. As my blushes seemed to feed the newcomer's desire to embarrass me, dislike turned to revulsion. This new situation was disturbing enough, but when he began teasing me in the Academy playground – my former haven from the Cameron household – I was devastated. When Nigel not unnaturally began to spend more and more time in the new boy's company, I took refuge in my attic room where, for some inexplicable reason, I spent most of my time peering into the mirror rehearsing crushing rejoinders against projected teasing by my 'tormentor'.

During this unhappy period, I received my first visit from Meg. She looked very grown-up in her carefully applied make-up and high heels. She took me to the cinema across the river to see 'The Loves of Carmen'. She bought two Mars Bars and two Crunchies in the foyer, then, after realising she hadn't left herself with enough money to get home, she sold them at half-price to a lady in the cloakroom. I found her behaviour strange. Was my Meg feckless? Yes she was, for when we left the cinema she decided she would walk home after all, and with the few pence left in her purse, treated me to a cup of tea in a nearby café.

When I told her how much the new boy's teasing distressed me, she almost exploded with anger – whether at him or me I wasn't sure. "Damn you, Jound," she said, "Where's your spunk? You can fell a grown man. Thump him." As far as my being banned from Culantryre was concerned, her advice was equally controversial. "When the holidays come round, just pack your case and go."

The tinderbox was primed and it only needed one spark to set it alight. Although Meg was slim, she had a buxom figure, which she emphasised by wearing fitting sweaters. Despite my youth, I too had a buxom figure. When the new boy made reference to our build, something inside me snapped. Thumping him would still leave me trapped where I didn't want to be. There was a better solution. I ignored the voice which repeated Willie's words to "Hang on," I was in no mood to rationalise. I had had enough. I wanted out, and out I was determined to go.

Two days after the Academy closed for the Christmas holidays, I packed my school case with clean underwear, textbooks and Xmas presents for everyone at Culantyre and hid the case outside. I spent the rest of the day fearful in case someone would find it before darkness descended and yet also excited at the thought of escaping. After tea, while I was meant to be washing the dishes, I slipped outdoors, retrieved the case and crept round to the front gate. As soon as my feet touched the pavement I started to run and didn't stop until I reached the bus station. I was just in time for the evening bus. When I climbed on board I made for the anonymity of the back seat, convinced that if anyone looked at me they would see how deceitful and evil I was.

It was not a pleasant journey. One of my legs shook uncontrollably. I was bewildered and confused. All I could be sure of was that I was heading back to the hills and fields where I had been happy, and where I wasn't constantly on edge, feeling nervous and unwanted. A wave of self-pity intermingled with my fear of being apprehended by the police. All my dreams were shattered. I couldn't understand what had gone wrong. Then I recalled the lady who had declined to take me in because she had felt I would be too clever to fit into her household. She had been a wise woman after all.

When the bus arrived at the Chapel on the main road, the driver seemed surprised Willie was not there to meet me. "You'll probably meet half-way towards Culantyre," he said. Then with a cheery "Goodnight," he drove off into the darkness. For a few moments I stood undecided what to do. On the bus I had decided not to inflict myself on the Milnes after all, but to live in the hills during the day and creep into the byre at night to sleep. I had convinced myself I could catch rabbits and support myself. But as I looked towards the dark, silent hills, I was far from confident. I plodded through the snow towards Culantyre, my mind in a whirl. What should I do? Before long my cold, wet feet began to feel very painful and the idea of living in the hills seemed less and less attractive with each step.

When I was within one or two hundred yards of the house, I could pick out a thin stream of pink light glinting through the trees. I stopped, still undecided whether or not I should throw myself on Jeanie's mercy or make for the byre. I put my case down and looked around me. I knew every inch and cranny of the land before me. The familiar outlines of favourite trees and boulders hypnotised me. I looked towards the river that had claimed my Bunty and listened to her scooshing noises as she jostled against her restrictive banks. She was in full spate. I felt cold and shivery. I looked upwards at the silent and emotionless stars twinkling above me. Every so often a wispy cloud would cover several of those watching eyes and I stood mesmerised by the vastness of something I couldn't understand. No longer aware of my cold, painful feet, I felt as if I was enveloped in a warm, invisible blanket. I was at one with the river, the trees and the mysterious night world that belonged to the animals. I could live off this land. It would support me willingly. But when my eyes wandered from the stars towards the slumbering outlines of the hills away in the distance, fear broke the spell and twinkling, mysterious stars or not, I was going home to Jeanie. I picked up my suitcase and half-ran, half-stumbled towards the beckoning pink light.

My arrival bordered on the farcical. A few minutes before I knocked on the door, Jeanie had let the sheepdog Mona out for a run. When she heard my knock, she thought it was Mona scratching to get back in, opened the door and was confronted with my unexpected figure. She let out a piercing scream and jumped backwards. Not expecting this welcome, I also screamed and jumped backwards. Upon hearing the commotion, Cathy crept downstairs, grabbed a heavy walking stick and was preparing to bring it down on my head when Jeanie gasped, "My goodness, it's Jound."

Moments later, I was inside, sobbing my heart out and trying unsuccessfully to put my deeds into some sort of logical order. Willie sat shuffling uncomfortably in his chair. He had never seen me so upset and didn't know how to cope with it. Jeanie, however, took it all in her stride. She dried my tears, gave me a pair of dry socks to change into, set a meal before me and told me I could tell her all about it in the morning, but meanwhile I should eat. So, although it was very late, I tucked into the three-course meal Jeanie had intuitively kept warm, for whom she couldn't explain.

Every time I heard a noise outside, I jumped. I was terrified the police would come and take me back to the Camerons. "Over my dead body," growled Willie. "I don't care who comes. No-one will disturb you this night." Tears of gratitude flowed. As always, I could rely on Willie. Here I was safe and loved.

Tonight there would be no standing in front of a candlelit mirror in an attic practising endless verbal defences against real or imaginary foes. Tonight I would sleep. I was back with my own folk.

Jeanie made up a makeshift bed next to Cathy and we lay in the dark holding hands until she fell asleep. It must have been about 3 a.m. when I heard the loud knock. Willie opened the door and my straining ears picked out the word 'police'. The stranger (an assumption on my part, for if he was a local man then Willie would know him) was invited in. As they moved into the kitchen I heard Willie say, "Before we get anywhere on this, you can take it from me that the child will not leave this house tonight or any other night until I know just what's going on."

About half-an-hour later, the policeman took his leave. After apologising for disturbing the Milnes at such a late hour I heard him say, "Aye, you're right Mr. Milne. I wouldn't like to be responsible if the wee lass did something stupid. I'll leave it to you and the Corporation to sort it out." Then he was off. I relaxed. He had left without me. Within minutes my tension and fear dissolved and I fell into a much-needed sleep.

I awoke the following morning to find I was alone in the bedroom. When I went downstairs there was no sign of Cathy or the other girls, only Willie pretending to be busy with some forms. After I had breakfasted, Jeanie asked me to explain what had upset me enough to make me behave so out of character. I couldn't put my finger on it. I babbled on about feeling unwelcome, how I couldn't seem to do anything to please the Camerons, how I felt strangely disconnected from everyone like I had felt at Foresthall and how desperately unhappy I felt all the time. I didn't mention how much the new boy's teasing distressed and embarrassed me – for that very reason – it embarrassed me

The Milnes listened to my incoherent rambling, and because they knew me so well, were able to separate the wheat from the chaff and pinpoint the problem. The very thing I hoped would help me get on in life – my education – was being dismissed as an affectation. Willie promised they wouldn't let me go until the Corporation found a place for me in the hostel. He was still rather annoyed that they hadn't done this in the first pace. "Too damn simple for them," he muttered angrily.

Communications flew back and forth between Culantyre and the Corporation, but by the end of the school holidays no solution had been reached. During the holidays I had carried on with my studies, pouring over the school books I had brought with me. Now I began to lose heart. There was probably no room in the hostel and I would never return to the Academy. To pass the time, I started to write a detective story in my red hardback Latin exercise book.

I think it was a Saturday when they came. Cathy and I were down in one of the far fields, searching through the muddy cart tracks for signs of glow-worms. These luminous beetles were most elusive. I had only seen them at night when they shone like diamonds in the moonlight and I was determined to see what they looked like in broad daylight – rather like looking for a needle in a haystack. When I heard my name being shouted by one of the new girls, I knew they had come. Panic flooded through me. Willie was away tending the sheep on a neighbouring farm. Would Jeanie be able to cope without him? I walked slowly back to the house. When I entered the kitchen, two men were sitting on the edge of the sofa and Jeanie was looking flustered. My back stiffened.

Only one of the strangers spoke. He politely explained he was from the Education Department and, as I must attend school, he had come to take me back to Inverness. I chewed my cheek. Jeanie intervened, saying I was most anxious to return to my schooling but I didn't want to return to the Camerons. The silent man looked uncomfortable. The other man reassured Jeanie he would do everything in his power to get me into the hostel, but in the meantime I had to return, temporarily at least, to the Camerons. Jeanie, believing I would be found a place in the hostel within a short time, and intimidated by the threat of legal action if she didn't let me go, finally gave way. I, however, remained highly suspicious, very much aware that the second gentleman had been studiously avoiding my eyes.

There was nothing I could do. I packed my case with the few possessions I had brought with me and Jeanie handed me a brown paper bag filled with some of her baking. When we reached the door Jeanie hugged me tightly, her lips trembling and tears filling her blue eyes. "God be with you, Jound. Don't give up," she whispered. I held her close to me for the first time in my life, trying desperately to control my shaking body, then silently I followed the two strangers to the gate. I turned to say goodbye but no words came. I swallowed repeatedly for I felt as if I had a lump in my throat. Through a watery haze I could just make out Jeanie's blurred blue shape. The pain in my chest and throat was excruciating as I tried once more to say goodbye, but again no noise came. Oh, the agony of that silent parting. I gave a little shrug and turned away. I followed the men who had come for me, a subdued, defeated figure and through my tears the blurred cart track reminded me of the snow-covered drive I had so defiantly marched up five years ago at Glenholm. I no longer felt strong and invincible. I was beaten. I uttered not a single word during our journey to Inverness.

When we arrived at the Camerons, the man from the Education Department left me with his quiet companion (probably a representative from Glasgow Corporation), who ushered me into the plush rarely used front parlour, where, as I had anticipated, was another representative of Glasgow Corporation. In front of Peggy, he lectured me about my behaviour and the trouble I had caused. I listened in silence, displaying no emotion whatsoever. When he asked me to explain myself, believing he had used the Education Department to do his 'dirty work' I remained silent. Exasperated by my attitude, he eventually said something to the effect that the Cameron's were right, I was an uppity little madam. Still I remained silent. When both men left, no doubt believing that they had done their duty, I was sent to bed. I lay awake for hours wondering why I couldn't fit in like Marie and Nigel, but couldn't come up with an answer. All I knew was that something inside me had died – something that was necessary for all-round growth. Eventually, I turned on my side, muttered "I don't care," and went to sleep.

The following morning I came downstairs to find I had been sent to Coventry – not even the children were allowed to speak to me. In retaliation, I stopped washing any clothes that were not mine. In the following weeks I lived a strange Jekyll and Hyde existence. In the morning I left a silent, sullen house and walked across the road into a world of laughter and noise. At the end of the school day the process was reversed. I kept up an outward appearance of normality at school and a defiant posture at home. But eventually my armour was pierced. I was standing in the playground surrounded by several of my classmates when one of the older girls approached me. "Excuse me," she said. "Are you Helen Hamilton?" "Yes," I replied, a shade defensively. "You don't know me," she continued, "but I know what's going on in your house and I think it's disgusting." Had she heard something from the new boy? It didn't matter. Unable to cope with this support, I fled to the toilets where I sat on one of the seats, crammed a handkerchief into my mouth and sobbed uncontrollably.

I was still there when one of my teachers pushed the toilet door open. The bell had gone, and concerned that I may have taken off again, she had come looking for me. After I had composed myself, she led me into a small room where I tried to explain the circumstances in my foster home and how unhappy I was. She reassured me it wasn't wicked or uppity to want to attend University. It was laudable. She also pointed out that the Camerons, who were much older than the Milnes, had probably been brought up in an environment where University education was considered a luxury. As for the teasing, it was quite natural for teenage boys. The trick was to throw it back. She promised nothing but suggested I give her a few days to think over my problem.

Two days later, Peggy came into my room and informed me that she had been approached by a teacher who was concerned about my education. She apologised for not understanding how much importance I attached to it, but now that she did, she was very anxious I settle down and get on with my studies. She suggested that if I put the last few weeks behind me everything would be as before. I nodded in agreement, but in reality mainly to get rid of her because I felt most uncomfortable with her sitting beside me on the bed – not because it was she, but because I always became uncomfortable if anyone stood or sat close to me.

After she had left, I sat for a long time weighing up the pros and cons of the situation. I did so much want to stay at the Academy, but I didn't want to stay with the Camerons. I knew the Corporation would never let me live in the hostel. The solution therefore lay in being fostered to someone else in Inverness or being returned to Glasgow where there were lots of senior secondary schools and where I would be near father. I made my mind up. I didn't want to stay. When I went downstairs I was greeted with false smiles and embarrassed "hullos." I did not respond. Even if I was capable of turning my emotions on and off, I had nothing I wanted to say. A week later I was 'removed'.

7

CHAPTER SEVEN
Wrong Turning

I was placed in a home in Glasgow called Eversley, where I remained for a few weeks until another foster home was found for me in Dalbeattie, a small town in the south west of Scotland. My new foster parents, a man, and a middle-aged lady confined to a wheelchair, had, I believe, originally agreed to take in a child of about eight or nine.

As soon as I entered their immaculate two-bedroom bungalow, I realised my size, if not my age, had caught them by surprise. One did not need to look very far to see why - although only 5 ft 2 inches tall. I had the physique of a sixteen-year-old and a rather obvious thirty six inch bust. As their newly married daughter's plans to move out had either been postponed or cancelled, I would have to sleep in my foster parents' bedroom!

I didn't want to share a bedroom with a married couple. I had never slept in the same room as a man in my life, not even my father. I had never seen Willie without a shirt on, let alone in his underwear. I was numbed. During the last six months Glasgow Corporation had placed three children with Jeanie when she had agreed to take two. After being rejected by one potential foster parent, I had been touted round Inverness like a sack of potatoes only to end up with four elderly foster parents whose home was so full I had to share my bed with another girl and a woman in her seventies. Now, at this awkward time of puberty, I was expected to share a bedroom with a middle-aged man and his wife. I was beginning to wish I had failed my eleven-plus. I felt the old resentment rising. Were the employees of Glasgow Corporation paid a commission when they found foster places for the children in their care? It seemed the only explanation for such haphazard placements. Why hadn't they just placed me in the hostel? Unable to voice my feeling about this new placement, just as I had been unable to voice my feelings about life with the Camerons, I began to nurse a strong dislike and contempt for everyone in authority. Neither age nor power seemed to be a reliable indicator of wisdom.

Despite this being the most luxurious home I had been placed in, I was once again desperately unhappy – an unhappiness compounded by the fact that for the first time in my life I felt out of place, not only in my foster home, but at school. I was behind in my class work and this, combined with merciless teasing about my bust size, began to take its toll.

From time to time, I heaved deep involuntary sighs, which irritated the family. I resented the fact my foster parents didn't seem to understand that father couldn't, rather than wouldn't, look after me, and I was angry because the Corporation were so late in forwarding my pocket money that my foster parents were out of pocket until it came through. Cause and effect - I don't know. But my whole personality seemed to disintegrate. I started to tell the most outrageous lies at school, claiming I had written several children's stories under a pseudonym. Naturally, as I couldn't provide my classmates with my pseudonym, no one believed me. But worse, much worse was to come.

On Saturdays I did the housework, which included the daughter's bedroom where she kept a small jug in which she saved silver threepenny and sixpenny pieces. One day I dipped my hand into the jug and stole sixpence. With the stolen money I bought three large buns. I dipped my hand into that jar again and again, stealing about three shillings in all.

My theft came to light in a rather strange way. When I was given my pocket money, I did as Jeanie had taught me – set aside some for a rainy day. This money was always considered sacrosanct. On this eventful day, I decided there was no point in saving for anything. I cashed my post office saving stamps, bought some sweets and went to the pictures. A friend of my foster parents saw me there and relayed this sighting to them. Surprised at my conspicuous spending, they demanded to know where I had got the money. Now a strange thing occurred. I would have been severely reprimanded by Jeanie for spending my savings, so instead of telling them I had cashed my saving stamps, I said I had been treated to the pictures by one of the girls at school. My story was checked out and found to be untrue. The jar in the bedroom was checked and found to be short. I was almost relieved at having been caught.

After I was given a lecture about my dishonesty, everyone promised to forgive me. But I couldn't forgive myself. The guilt consumed me. I couldn't understand what on earth was happening to me. I hated and despised myself; detested the very sound of my name. I could think of only one solution. I must make for Glasgow and find my father. All this moving about and misbehaving had to stop. I wanted to feel the way I had felt at Culantyre. And so one afternoon I set off to follow the railway line to Glasgow. Perhaps father could find a place for me with one of his friends. Perhaps my Meg, who was now living with an Aunt in Glasgow, could persuade her to take me too. Perhaps, perhaps….

I followed the road running parallel with the railway track until the track disappeared. In the hope that the road would eventually catch up with the railway lines, I kept on going, but after a few hours I gave up. I was lost and tired. I tried to hitch a lift back to the town from which I had fled but no one would stop for me. So I promptly lay down on the grass verge and pretended I had fainted. My ruse worked. An alarmed gentleman stopped. He drove me back to my foster parents who called the doctor. He pronounced me fit, which physically I was. At their wits end, my foster parents asked that I be removed, and despite the guilt and shame I felt at my behaviour I felt as if a weight had been lifted from my shoulders.

My escort back to Glasgow was once again a plump lady. I cannot remember if it was the same lady I had met before, but it didn't really matter. By now I disliked anyone who worked for Glasgow Corporation.

When the chauffeur asked if the foster parents would take another child, she replied "Never again. This one was enough to put them off for life. There are two of them you know, but this one is by far the worst." I had to agree with her. I was certainly not the child who had left Culantyre. I had become a cunning, evil monster, of that I was sure. Nevertheless, the cunning, evil monster silently prayed it wouldn't be fostered again, for somewhere at the back of its mind it was beginning to realise that living closely with people, especially when sharing either their bed or their bedroom, caused it to behave in a distressing manner.

We were in the driveway when I recognised where I was. "I've been here before," I volunteered. "Not here you haven't," said the plump lady. "You would have learned to behave yourself if you had." It was Foresthall.

I was left there about 2 p.m. This time there was no trailing round high fences and stone walls as I had done some five years previously with my Meg. By 3 p.m. I had tucked some comics under my arm, climbed over the wall and was heading for the nearest shops. I sold the comics to a small second-hand bookshop, bought ten Woodbine, a box of Swan Vestas matches and went to the cinema. In the anonymity of the dimly lit hall, I lit my first cigarette and nearly choked to death. I didn't try to smoke another. Nevertheless, I held on to the symbols of my 'maturity' for several weeks before flushing them down the toilet.

The following morning I again climbed over the wall - this time to search for my Meg. I knew the street where she lived but not the number. Unfortunately I didn't know my aunt's surname, which made my search even more difficult. Towards lunchtime I decided to buy some chips and think through my situation. Minutes after leaving the fish and chip shop, I was approached by a man in his late thirties or early forties. He murmured a few inaudible words. I said

"Pardon," but before he could respond I heard the raised and angry voice of my Meg. She did not mince her words. She accused the stranger of trying to pick up a thirteen-year-old schoolgirl. He apologised repeatedly, asserting he thought I was much older, but Meg kept directing his attention towards my heavy school shoes and ankle socks. Finally, embarrassed by the crowd which was now gathering, he took to his heels and ran.

I spent several hours with Meg, during which time my whole body seemed to unwind, particularly my jaws, which recently always seemed to be clenched. I didn't have to put on an act; didn't have to try and please everyone; didn't see a need to lie. Nothing was under attack. I had nothing to defend and I chatted and laughed as if I had never stopped doing either.

Meg had a date for the evening, so I could only stay until 6 p.m. As she dressed and made-up for her night out, I got caught up in the excitement of her preparations. I found the intricacies of applying make-up fascinating. But as I watched I realised my Meg had changed. Her voice was different. She spoke with a broad Glaswegian accent and her phraseology was not that of former years. She was not progressing. She was going backwards. Her beautiful rosy cheeks were now pale and her thin, sensitive hands shook as she held a cigarette in one and a lipstick in the other. Only her hair remained unchanged. It still shone like copper glinting in the sun. As she rambled on about boys and dancing I felt a strange sadness. I had lost my Meg, as I had lost my parents – slowly. There would be no help here.

We were, in a strange way, exact opposites. She had never fallen foul of the Corporation, but she had lost the battle. I kept making one disastrous move after another, yet in some things I was determined to 'hang on'.

Whenever our Aunt entered the room I noticed Meg's attitude towards her was almost submissive. When my Aunt finally left to visit some friends, Meg confided in me that she was unemployed and owed our Aunt several weeks' rent. For these reasons she could not ask my Aunt to take me in too. I said it didn't matter. After all, I had only two more years to go now that I wouldn't be going to university. Meg then gave me some money and instructions on how to get the tram back to Foresthall.

In the tram I did some serious thinking. What had happened to my Meg? Why was she unemployed? Was it because she was lazy? Maybe she didn't like doing the repetitive jobs to which she was limited because she was uneducated or unskilled. But my Meg was not only intelligent, she was of above average intelligence. Had she given up, or had she by returning to her roots, condemned herself to repeating the life cycle of our parents? My mind went round and round. Somewhere in there lay part of the answer. What was the missing essential that had turned my Meg into a submissive loser? I was confused.

Had I taken an easy route and also given up? The thought was unbearable but it had to be examined. When I had finished examining my life I was determined on several points. I would never lie again, no matter what the cost, and never, never again, would I steal. I had thrown away my chance of a good education but somehow I would make up for it. What I now needed to do was reclaim my faith in myself and that included fighting to hang on to whatever dignity I possessed. Unfortunately, my idea of dignity included a vow never to be submissive.

Consoled or duped by these ruminations, I sauntered nonchalantly back into Foresthall only to be met by an extremely irate nurse who irritably demanded, "Where the hell have you been?" I replied that I had been to see my sister. Apparently, while I was away, someone from the Corporation had called to take me to another placement, "And where were you – at your sister's," the nurse exploded. "Well," I replied, slowly and coolly, "had I known she was coming I would have made myself available to her." This was not quite the answer the nurse expected. And she raised her hand as if to hit me. Something in my eyes, however, stopped her hand mid-way, which was just as well. Vowing never to lie or steal was one thing. Allowing a stranger to assault me without retaliating was quite another.

The following day the Children's Officer returned, and as we drove away from Foresthall I glanced along the wall I had breached so easily. Nothing but respect would hold me now - my respect for other people and their respect for me. Both would be hard earned.

8

CHAPTER EIGHT
Lay By

I was returned to Eversley, the home in which I had spent a few weeks prior to my last foster placement. Never was the sight of stark dormitories and highly polished floors more welcome. After I was introduced to Matron, I was taken along to the playroom to mingle with people of my own circumstances. I immediately felt as if an unwelcome spotlight, which had been trained on me, had suddenly been turned off. At lunch time I tucked voraciously into my food, no longer feeling guilty that my healthy appetite would eat into whatever, if any, profits were made from fostering me.

I felt I had returned home, was in the surroundings where I was most at ease. At night I stretched out in my bed and savoured the joy of not having to pretend I was asleep, look the other way or pull the blankets over my head when anyone climbed in or out of bed. Eyes which had been blinkered with adolescent embarrassment, could now look in any direction without anxiety. It was lovely. I had not realised just how much discomfort I had experienced while sharing a bedroom with my former foster parents. Anonymity brought me peace.

Eversely was situated in a rather select suburb of Glasgow and catered for some twenty or thirty children of all ages. The boys and girls were segregated into small dormitories upstairs, whilst the babies and infants slept downstairs. We had access to all the rooms in the home with the exception of the staff quarters. There was discipline, but it was not intrusive, for when you know the rules they become a part of your way of life.

Slowly, I began to feel less defensive and in a desperate attempt to redeem myself, I ploughed all my energies into polishing the floors – upstairs and down – until they gleamed. My work did not go unnoticed, for the Assistant Matron gave me 1/6d every week for my efforts, but more important, she praised my handiwork. The tight, cold feeling which had invaded my body for so long, began to melt, and as I rubbed away at the linoleum with the heavy buck, I even began to sing to myself.

Apart from polishing the floors, I had another distraction. As there were several infants under the age of two, the nurses welcomed any help they could get, and I soon became a frequent visitor to the nursery. I loved washing and feeding the babies. An amazing tenderness would flow out from me as I sprinkled sweet-smelling talcum in the creases of their smooth, plump flesh.

I became particularly fond of a little girl called Allison. Unlike the rest of the babies, she responded to the sound of my voice. Whenever I changed her nappy, her arms would jerk upwards and wave about as she tried to touch my mouth and eyes. In order that I might spend more time playing with her, I always kept her to the last. As she sat on my lap I would talk softly and lovingly to her and she would reward me with soft cooing noises to which I responded with more soft whisperings and nuzzlings.

Unfortunately Allison responded too well to my 'mothering'. When I wasn't there she began to cry for attention. I was told I was spoiling her; she was becoming too demanding and I must stop seeing her. I knew the nurses were right, but it hurt dreadfully.

When she was taken along to the playroom, I would watch her from a distance. Compared with the other toddlers, she was quite precocious. Whenever she mastered a new skill, her eyes would turn towards the nurse in attendance, but as often as not, her new accomplishment went unheeded. I would feel a terrible sorrow tugging at my chest. My love had aroused her expectations far beyond the level that the nurses were able to fulfil. It was not that I had loved her too much or the nurses too little, it was simply that no matter how devoted they were, the nurses didn't have time to give her individual attention.

Deprived of Allison's company, I turned my attentions elsewhere and spent hours on the back lawn doing physical exercises. It was my party piece to jump off a table and land on the ground doing the splits, or to do the splits suspended between two chairs. Naturally, all this exercise built up my leg muscles and it was my proud, if less than feminine boast, that I could crush a grown man to death with my thighs – an assertion that sent the boys into body-shaking fits of laughter – laughter which was lost on me. I was still an innocent as far as the opposite sex was concerned. No pangs or desires ever invaded my body; smutty jokes were never repeated in my presence, and I shared no girlish secrets with anyone. I was a tomboy through and through.

If I lacked feminine wiles, however, there was nothing masculine about my figure. The sight of my somewhat curvaceous body jumping and rolling all over the garden proved too much for Matron, who one day drew me aside and suggested it was time I wore some support. I couldn't understand what needed supporting. My stomach was flat and muscular and my breasts, although large, were young enough to defy the laws of gravity.

My introduction to the wearing of support was hilarious. Matron had found a huge, wicker basket full of an assortment of old fashioned brassieres and corsets in the clothing store – apparently they had been donated to the home by a charity. In me she found a way of putting them to use. I must confess I was more than a little perplexed as to how one put on a brassiere, and it took several attempts before I managed to figure out how the straps and hooks worked. When I finally managed to put the wretched and voluminous garment on I was disappointed, for to say the least, it was more covering than supporting.

If I found the brassieres ludicrous, the corsets left me in hysterics. Not only did they lace up the front, but they also had large protruding studs. I found this new pink armour very uncomfortable and restrictive, particularly when I bent down. Matron assured me I would become accustomed to wearing it and insisted that within a few weeks I wouldn't even notice I was wearing a corset. I was not convinced, but already I could see that the corsets at least could provide me with some fun. Within minutes of covering them with a cotton dress I rushed outside, approached a group of the boys and invited them to punch me hard in the stomach. Only one took up the challenge. He winked mischievously at the other boys and then aimed a blow at my abdomen. My muscles and the studs withstood the punch but a puzzled lad was left clutching his bruised knuckles - so much for my being a genteel lady.

When this story reached Matron's ears, she whisked me off to John Street where the Corporation supplied me with several beautifully embroidered brassieres, but happily, no corsets. When I returned home, I sneaked a furtive look at myself in the mirror. I was pleased with what I saw. There was nothing tomboyish about my reflection. I looked feminine and quite shapely. Femininity was something I had never thought about before. Although I had often played with the boys at Boleskine Primary School, those games had been limited to shinty or wrestling. As I always played to win, there was no question of displaying femininity on the field, neither did the boys give any indication that I was other than one of them. In my thirteenth year I was still unaware that boys were indeed the opposite sex. I tended to look upon them all as brothers, a view reinforced by living so closely amongst them in various institutions. Even today I still have difficulty in separating males from females. I tend to treat them the same.

If I had a somewhat neutral attitude towards males as such, there was one place where I did feel feminine stirrings. We were regularly treated to outings to the Empire Theatre in Glasgow, where I watched with envy as slim, supple dancers, dressed in satins and chiffon, performed magical dance routines. In the darkness I dared to dream that when I grew up I too would be supple and slim, wear beautiful clothes and my beauty and grace overawe men. In my fantasies, men only appeared as distant admirers. That they should become an integral part of my life had no place in my daydreams.

How wonderful is childhood, for only then can we say, "When I grow up I will…" and add anything to that phrase knowing that no one can say whether or not we will achieve our desires. Fortunately I did not know that I had already reached my maximum height; that my short legs would never lengthen; my pale cheeks become rosy or that I would carry with me for the rest of my life a complete lack of dress sense. All of these, when combined with an irrepressible sense of humour, ensured that I would never be sophisticated.

As well as those wonderful visits to the theatre, Matron occasionally took two or three of us at a time to Wendy's, a city centre restaurant. I loved those excursions into town. Dressed in my best outfit, I would sit primly at the table and watch the other diners, anxious to learn how they, the normal people, held their knives and forks and sipped their tea or coffee. But mostly I listened. Voices intrigued me. I was very careful to pronounce my words properly and was forever on guard against picking up sloppy speech, such as pronouncing 'going' as 'goin', 'bird' as 'burd' or 'film' as 'filum', all of which are common Glaswegian pronunciations.

As the months passed I thought I was settling in quite well. I was sent to Albert Drive Academy, although whether during or after the spring term I cannot remember – probably because as a result of epidemics of mumps, measles or chickenpox, I actually spent very little time there. On Saturdays, after we had received our pocket money, we either went to the cinema, window-shopping or to a local park where we fished for minnows. I have pleasant memories of walking through the park in the company of younger children as the sun shone out of a cloudless sky. I cannot remember any display of inflexible regimentation or cruelty of any sort, either physical or mental.

Sometime during the summer holidays, Matron gave me permission to visit my sister. Meg was waiting for me when I arrived at my Aunt's, but instead of taking me to the pictures, as I had anticipated, she took me to see my mother whom I hadn't seen for six or seven years. I could hardly contain my excitement as long-repressed thoughts surfaced. Would she look like me? Would her house be neat and clean? Would she ask me to live with her now that I no longer needed constant attention? My head was in such a whirl; I couldn't make up my mind whether to call her mother or mum. Both words seemed so strange, so difficult to say.

When we left the tram I was uncomfortably aware that we were in an area which could aptly be described as a slum. I felt conspicuous in my clean, expensive clothing, which drew the attention of several people in the street. Panic tingled from my atlas to my coccyx as I prayed mother's house would not be like the one Dad had taken us to at the end of the war. Images of fly-encrusted papers flashed on and off in my mind. I tried to console myself with the conviction that mother would keep her house neat and tidy no matter what her surroundings, but my conviction weakened when we entered mother's close and I took in the peeling paintwork, the litter-strewn passageway and the strong smell of urine.

Meg knocked on a brown, wooden door. When it opened a smell of soap and rotten wood escaped into the close. The small, plump lady holding on to the door handle said "Hullo." I stared quizzically at her. Meg realised I didn't recognise her. "Good heavens, Jound," she said accusingly, "This is your mother." I took in the pale, worry-lined face; the sparse grey hair piled on top of her head; the blood-shot eyes and the welcoming but toothless smile. I was astounded. Could this worn out woman be my mother – she of the white marble skin and large blue eyes? Without realising what I was doing, I stretched out my hand and politely said, "Pleased to meet you," but the word 'mother' stuck in my throat. Taken aback, she glanced quickly at Meg before stretching out her hand to grasp mine. Neither of us displayed any emotion.

As I sat motionless on one of the chairs facing a coal fire, I took in the torn, grease-spotted wallpaper and the cracked linoleum devoid of any pattern except round the skirting board where no feet had trod. A shaky gate-legged table stood in front of the window which overlooked the back court. Its green oilcloth covering was splattered with crumbs and tea stains. I was digesting all this information, shuffling it into order, when a movement behind me interrupted my thoughts. I twisted round and peered into the dark bed recess. My heart turned over. The thin, emaciated body lying on the bed was that of a man. Horrified, I turned towards Meg. She answered my unspoken question by explaining the man was an invalid and the owner of the house. In return for mother looking after him, he allowed her the sole use of the bedroom.

I felt cheated. I had wanted my first meeting with mother to be a private affair. Instead, there was a stranger lying in the recess probably listening to every word I said. My back stiffened and no matter how hard I tried, my ensuing conversation was far removed from the mother-daughter conversation I had visualised. Mother however, gave no indication that she sensed my discomfort, but continued stirring a pan of curried mince, which she was heating on an old gas stove. She eventually served the mince up in cracked soup plates. As there were not enough knives and forks to go round, I ate mine with a spoon, struggling with each spoonful not to gag.

As we talked, the guilt I felt at finding the house so untidy slowly subsided and in its place a strange sadness, an almost peaceful sadness, crept over me. I realised mother and I were strangers - not because of the passage of time, but because of the difference in our lifestyles. For years I had longed for her, wanted to be held in her arms and to share laughter and tears with her. Now I felt I had outgrown her.

I had seen so many wonderful things she had not seen, or ever would see. I had observed so many sides to life and living that when I was able to support myself I would have a true choice. My parents, on the other hand, had known only poverty. They had never had the opportunity to be educated to secondary level, had seemingly lacked the will-power or knowledge to help themselves, and, like so many similarly trapped, had turned to alcohol for escape. The most difficult thought to cope with was the fact that by deserting me they had given me a far greater opportunity to grow and blossom than I would have had with them. Not an easy thought to face at thirteen, for it casts doubt on the very bonds of parenthood. But I could not escape from this truth. Nothing seen or heard is ever unseen or unheard. But if ever there was a day in my life I would wish to eradicate from my memory, this was it

As Meg and mother chatted away, unaware of my analytical ruminations, I felt like a Judas. I wanted to cry out, "Stop. Please stop talking. I am deceiving you with my nods and smiles. Forgive my arrogance, my complacency, my nice clean clothes, but most of all forgive me for not being able to help you." But I remained silent, kept up my pretence as I acted out the role of a long lost daughter.

When we had finished eating, mother suggested we go for a walk round the local market. I reluctantly agreed – reluctantly because I was ashamed of her shabby clothes and stockingless, fire-marked legs. She, however, was obviously very proud of me, eagerly introducing me to friends she met on our journey. When she bought me a pair of white canvas sandals I felt dreadful. I knew she was spending more than she could afford. When she bought several sixpenny love stories, I thanked her profusely, but as I grasped the shiny, vulgar covers, they only seemed to emphasise just how far apart we were. When she asked me to pay a return visit, I promised to come the following week, but my mind was already made up. I didn't want to come back. My decision was made less distressing by the fact that she also suggested that when I left school I should come to live with her. It was well known in institutions that parents who deserted their children often re-appeared the year before they left school to start work. I convinced myself that this was why I really didn't want to visit her again. It was easier to blame her for something she probably hadn't even thought of, than for me to admit I found her way of life unacceptable.

When I returned to Eversley I told everyone how beautiful and refined my mother was and I showed off my new sandals to anyone who was interested. The romantic novellas, however, I tore up and flushed down the toilet. When I had left Foresthall I had promised I would never cry again and I had also vowed never to lie again. On this day I had lied to my own mother, and that night the tears sneaked from between my sleepless eyelids and bumped accusingly down my burning cheeks. I wished the ground would open up and swallow me. It wasn't that I didn't love her; just that I could no longer relate to her. The squalor of her surroundings not only appalled, but frightened me. I never wanted to live like that. I had seen Meg change, revert to the behaviour patterns of our roots. I didn't want to change. When I finally fell asleep, I wandered into a nightmare of poverty, collapsing houses and scuttling, nibbling rats. When I woke the following morning to find myself safe in my clean bed, surrounded by polished floors and clean windows, through which the sun shone, I felt temporarily grateful to Glasgow Corporation.

That visit to mother had several consequences, none of which I immediately connected to that dreadful day. The immediate result was insomnia. As I lay awake trying desperately to sleep, I found the heavy breathing of one of the girls extremely annoying. With a total lack of consideration for her sleep, I would prod the offending girl awake and tell her to "stop making that din or else." Not unnaturally, she resented this interference with her sleep, just as I had resented Meg's interference with mine so many years before. I was becoming a bully. I became quarrelsome and uncooperative and for some strange reason, went on a hunger strike because Matron wouldn't let me go potato picking with the rest of the school. On the third day, after Matron promised to let me spend a week at Culantyre, I called off my strike. But it had merely been a ruse and my promised trip never materialised.

I was still in a state of inner turmoil when Meg visited me. She was very angry with me for not keeping my appointment with mother. When I could not give her a satisfactory explanation for my behaviour she flounced off, but not before telling me that from now on both she and mother would consider me dead. I found the emotional trauma too much and rather than struggle with conflicting emotions, which I could not reconcile, banished them both effectively from my mind. A new pattern had been set. In future, whenever someone I loved hurt me, I would cut him or her from my consciousness as a surgeon would cut away a tumour.

The staff were totally unaware of my distress. It was not common practice to discuss emotional traumas with them. All they knew was what they could see. I had apparently upset my sister and I was aggressive and bullying. Matron quite rightly decided it would be in the interests of the other children, as well as my own, if I was removed to another home where there would be children of my own age.

9

CHAPTER NINE
Cul De Sac

7. Castlemilk home - impressive exterior, depressive interior.

I was sent to Castlemilk, a large home on the outskirts of Glasgow, which was isolated from the rest of the world by its vast, secluded grounds.

As we approached the building along a beautiful tree-lined driveway, the sun shone through the leaves of the tall chestnut trees, creating such variations in light that the moving, leafy canopy overhead reminded me of the view down a kaleidoscope. At that moment it also occurred to me that my life also resembled the contents of a kaleidoscope, with patterns forming and reforming within strict boundaries. Was I fated to inhabit every home run by Glasgow

Corporation? Did my moves always have to be preceded by my strange ability to cause havoc? Oh, how I wished that particular fragment could be removed from my kaleidoscope. However, as I looked through the car window, I could see no havoc. The sun overhead was the same sun that had shone on my secret island at Culantyre. The gently moving leaves of the chestnut trees were as delicate as those on my Highland rowan trees, and the flowers growing in the woods grew with the same apparent random as those on Willie's moor. Thank goodness no one, not even I, could create enough havoc to destroy nature's self-perpetuating beauty.

I was allocated a bed in one of the dormitories radiating off the large square hall on the first floor, which was occupied by the older children, the younger ones having their own accommodation on the floor below. The staff occupied the top floor. Although there were two playrooms in the basement, they were dark, devoid of furniture, considered to be spooky and only used as a passageway to some other part of the basement. The older boys and girls, when not playing in the grounds, preferred to congregate in the first floor hall, which, although sparsely furnished, was heated by a large coal fire over which was a gigantic wooden carving of a battle scene apparently carved from a solid piece of wood. It was a magnificent piece of craftsmanship, which set off to perfection the warm wood panelling and the beautiful parquet floor.

My overall impression of my new home was of vastness and noise. The home catered for about fifty children, which made it impossible for the nursing staff to keep an eye on everyone and therefore allowed for a reasonable degree of freedom and anonymity. The toddlers were supervised in the adjoining purpose-built play hut, but the rest of us were free either to wander from floor to floor or play in the large grounds.

My first morning started off catastrophically. While handing out plates of porridge, one of the nurses slipped and spilt a plate of lumpy porridge over my head. I was ordered along to the scullery to wash up and there I met Mrs. McQuater, a part-time cleaner. She took one look at the burnt porridge lumps nestling on top of my head and offered to wash my hair. I took straight away to this plump, middle-aged woman with rosy, wrinkle-free cheeks and twinkling eyes. She reminded me of Jeanie.

In order to stay close to her, I offered to dry the breakfast and tea dishes and clean the dining-room. In return, she gave me some extra pocket money. Time spent with her was a revelation. She was full of stories about stroppy salesgirls, insolent tram conductors and the many and varied facets of everyday living outside the home. She also provided a welcome conduit for my observations about the home, its staff, the children and, later, my school.

For some strange reason, I was sent to a primary school in the grounds of the home. Whether this was to assess me or fill in the last months of the school term, I don't know. Eventually, however, I was sent to Queenspark Junior Secretary where, although now thirteen years of age, I was put in the first year. When I asked Matron why I had not been sent to a grammar school, she responded, "If the Corporation thought you were clever enough then they would have sent you to a grammar school." I didn't like her response but there was nothing I could do about it.

There was, however, something I could do about my pocket money. Everyone was allocated this according to his or her age and at that time I was entitled to 1/-d per week – 12 pence in pre-decimalization money. On my first Saturday I was handed a bar of chocolate worth four old pence – one third of the value of my pocket money! The following week I publicly and noisily declined the chocolate and insisted upon receiving my full allowance. This demand had three effects. Firstly, it convinced Matron that I was a troublemaker. Secondly, from that day on the older children were given the full value of the money due to them and, thirdly, we were allowed out on Saturday afternoons to spend it

My next encounter with Matron was more serious. When I was asked to join several of the older girls, who rose at six in the morning to help the night staff strip and make the beds, I readily agreed. In return for helping out, we were invited down to the basement kitchen where we were allowed to make as much toast and drink as much milk as we could consume. I loved these morning feasts not only for the opportunity to eat hot buttered toast, but because I liked listening to the adult conversations. I was always desperate to hear about the outside world, for we had no access to radios or newspapers.

One morning the fireman, who serviced the fire extinguishing equipment and who was on call for any emergencies which might occur during the night, rushed in and advised us to hide as Matron was on her way downstairs. The staff pushed us down a flight of narrow stone stairs into the bowels of the castle where the vegetables were stored. As we waited shivering among the turnips and carrots, I learned that the kitchen was strictly out of bounds even to those helping with domestic chores. Anxious not to be found in an out-of-bounds area, when we got the all-clear, I rushed up the stairs, two at a time, and bumped into Matron on her way back downstairs. She grabbed my arm and demanded to know where I had been. When I replied, "In the kitchen," she slapped me forcefully across the face. It was the wrong move. I allowed no one to hit me. I slapped her back and told her that if she ever raised a hand to me again I would kill her. Sounds dreadful, but how many times have you heard someone say, "I'll kill him," and known that the person uttering the threat had no intention of killing anyone. A few days later one of the boys confided in me that they had been warned not to antagonise me, as I was "a killer".

That night I could not sleep. I felt sure I would be moved again and the only place for a branded killer was prison. Could Matron have me sent to prison for slapping her? Perhaps. They seemed to be able to move children around so easily without a thought for the consequences or without independent adjudication. And why was I the only one to retaliate? I had seen Matron publicly lash out with her cane across the back of a nude girl, whose only response had been a pathetic but unsuccessful attempt to escape from her. Why had she not turned and fought back? Was it really acceptable for adults to cane or slap children indiscriminately? If so, what was wrong with me? Had someone caned me in the nude in the presence of boys I would have retaliated in kind. Was I a psychopath, evil to the core, or just someone prepared to challenge what I considered to be unacceptable behaviour? If the latter, then I was the only one prepared to do so.

By the time morning arrived, I was so confused I began to doubt my own reasoning. I was just a bad person; I had probably always been a bad person.

When I went to school I felt totally disconnected from my surroundings. Instead of seeing people, I saw things, or more precisely, my eyes concentrated on things – ankle socks clinging to scrubbed skin (I wore boys knee length socks turned down to look like ankle socks); fingernails with white half moons enhancing hands which looked long and delicate compared to mine; shining long hair plaited and tied with silk ribbons; blouse collars starched and ironed to a crisp perfection and faces which bore none of the sadness or confusion I felt. I heard the teacher call my name several times before I responded and when I again looked round the class, the socks, nails and hair fitted together again and I saw rows of girls, all of whom seemed prettier, neater and more self-confident than I. I looked down at my mature body, which looked somewhat incongruous in my gym-slip. Everything was false. I had been deluding myself for over a year. I was an evil nobody with aspirations far beyond my ability. And with my mind full of conflicting, fragmented memories, I let go.

As the months passed, deprived of intellectual stimulation either in the home or at school, I withdrew into myself, hiding from the sea of sadness which surrounded me.

There was 'Inga', so-called because that was the only word he could say. He spent most of his time running around naked from the waist down because, as well as being mentally handicapped, he was incontinent. Sometimes, when I spooned food into his gaping mouth, I felt sure he was trying to communicate, respond to my tenderness, but Inga was never given the time or attention to learn to communicate. He was frequently smacked for some perceived misdemeanour or another; and, confused and unable to understand why, he would cry 'Inga' over and over again. When I asked what would become of him when he grew up I was told not to worry about that as he would not live to adulthood. Poor Inga!

One of my most vivid memories is of a little boy who couldn't have been more than ten years old. After his mother had been murdered in a most gruesome manner, he and his older brother had been sent to Castlemilk. On this particular day he was taken out, either to go to court or to see a lawyer. When he returned one of the nurses asked him to show me what he had clenched in his hand. With his eyes sparkling and his face radiating pleasure at the good fortune that had come his way, he opened his fist and showed me three half-crowns. Someone had taken pity on him. I looked at the money then at his innocent smiling face. The enormity of what had happened had not yet sunk in. For the moment he was being given much needed attention but in a few months he would be on his own, one of fifty struggling to survive amidst the flotsam and jetsam, his particular sadness lost amidst so many others.

Unable to cope with the reality of all this sadness, I took refuge in dreams, for dreams were my only escape, and I began to live in a world of fantasy. Whereas I used to find it irksome to stop whatever I was doing to go to bed, now I couldn't wait for bedtime. All I wanted to do was curl up and sleep. I wanted silence. Complete and total silence. I wanted a little world of my own where other people's sadnesses did not intrude, and so bed became a haven.

Fortunately, during my stay in Castlemilk I had two things working in my favour. One was my friendship with Mrs. McQuater. She never failed to raise my flagging spirits and her little scullery became my confessional box and my stage, where with dramatic gestures and postures, I turned the day's events into comedies. The other was my friendly relations with my classmates. It was they who introduced me to permed hair, powder and lipstick – at least for one special occasion – the school Christmas dance. Somehow the class prefect had managed to persuade the school to allow the class to arrange their own party. We booked the hall, provided the food and soft drinks and invited our own guests, who naturally were all of the opposite sex. Mrs. McQuater treated me to a home perm and I was allowed to choose a party dress from the store.

When I joined the rest of the girls in the cloakroom I was stunned at how grown-up they looked in their sophisticated dresses and high heels. Needless to say I was the only one wearing a woollen long-sleeved dress, flat shoes and ankle socks. But they were as impressed with my figure as I was with their high heels. My dress may have been less glamorous but it emphasised a 36-21-35 figure, which under a gym-slip had looked matronly.

One of my classmates insisted upon making up my face, and when I saw the finished result, vanity crept into my body. I actually looked as pretty as most of my classmates, and for one glorious evening I felt like Cinderella. Of course there was no prospect of finding a boyfriend, even had I so wished. At first they surrounded me but when the word got round that I lived at Castlemilk their interest quickly evaporated. There was no point in having a girlfriend who was not allowed out.

Apart from my first school dance, I found the festive season at Castlemilk disturbing rather than exciting. This was probably due to the fact that I had outgrown the parties, the conjurers and organised games and viewed the frenetic activity with an almost analytical detachment. For me, those brief excursions outside the home merely emphasised the divide between 'me' and 'them', the normal people.

I was also aware that for a minority of the children their first Christmas away from home proved to be a traumatic experience. Some believed Santa would grant them their wish to return home; others that their parents would not leave them in Castlemilk over Christmas. Both groups were doomed to be disappointed – for not only did their absent parents not appear, more often than not they didn't even bother to send a letter or Christmas card. Some managed to hide their sadness. Others could be found lying prostrate on their beds, heads buried in their arms while presents, wrapping paper and string lay strewn on the floor where it had been kicked, not by an ungrateful child but by a child heart-broken that not one of them had come from 'home'. Sometimes, however, similar behaviour was occasioned by the fact that their presents, usually second-hand donations, were unsuitable either for their age or gender. Why this happened when mountains of toys were delivered to the home I could not fathom. But when I tell you my present was a large tin car, you will understand what I mean! It was such a wasteful practice. Most of the toys ended up in a huge bonfire.

There were of course parents who did visit their children at this time, but there were some who made appointments and did not turn up. How I hated them. Each time I saw a child sitting in the hall all dressed up waiting for Mum or Dad to call, I crossed my fingers and prayed they wouldn't be disappointed. But there was always someone who was; someone who, after his or her best clothes had been removed, retired to the bathroom to sob till he or she was exhausted.

If those walls could speak they would testify to how loyal those children were to their absent parents; how forgiving in their childish innocence. They would speak not of their weaknesses, but strengths – how behind the only door that locked, with no one for comfort, they bathed their wounds with salty tears. It made me angry. Not because it reminded me of Mary at Foresthall waiting for hours for her sister, but because the youngsters didn't demand parental love; they merely wanted their parents to accept the unquestioning love they had to offer.

For some of the children there was another traumatic experience in store. During this season of jollity and goodwill there was always an increase in the number of people volunteering to be 'Aunts' and 'Uncles'. That they were motivated by a genuine desire to share their home temporarily with an underprivileged child was indisputable, but the results were often more destructive than constructive.

For the child who could still communicate, still respond, these visits provided much needed support and gave them someone 'of their own' in whom to confide. Alas, for those whose emotions had become stunted and whose trust had been bruised and abused too often, they presented tremendous difficulties. Unable to respond quickly enough to sudden offerings of love and interest, their invitations to tea became fewer and fewer, until at last they stopped. I found it excruciating to watch such a child struggle once more to cope with rejection. Aggression, tantrums and withdrawal from the other children were the telltale signs. Then came the 'I don't care' period when all verbal approaches were dismissed and any form of touching was rejected. But they did care. They were just too young to understand that in a normal relationship love was a two-way thing. They had spent years loving someone who did not return their love. They did not know their Christmas Aunts and Uncles expected instantaneous signs of appreciation or gratitude. Neither did the adults understand that by persevering and making no emotional demands on the child they could one day reap a love that would touch them by its depth and simplicity

Odd the barriers to elastic thinking. I have known twenty-a-day smokers who cannot understand an alcoholic, and people with phobias they can avoid who cannot understand either agoraphobia or anxiety. I am quite sure that most people understand why a feral cat will not let you stroke it. Why then was it so difficult for those Christmas Aunts and Uncles, not to mention the authorities, to understand why unloved children, children deprived of personal attention, reacted the way they did!

Apart from the devastation these experiences caused, there was another unsettling side effect to the Aunt and Uncle scheme. In the forties and fifties, homes were very bleak places – dormitories resembled hospital wards and playrooms were invariably devoid of furniture except for a few dining-room chairs. Upholstered chairs or carpets were unknown – by the children at least.

Visiting a family home, even a modest one, merely emphasised this.

I remember being invited by a classmate to spend an afternoon with her family and being completely overwhelmed by the fitted carpets, upholstered suite, delicate china ornaments and the curtains – oddly enough it was the net curtains which fascinated me. At tea-time I joined the family round a table covered with a linen cloth, upon which stood floral china dishes containing a varied selection of foods, a floral china teapot encased in a multi-coloured woollen cosy and, most intriguing of all, a three-tiered cake stand artistically garnished with an assortment of fancy cakes. After tea I joined my friend in her bedroom, which of course, was furnished with a small suite, shelving for her books and toys and a clutter of all those things with which young teenagers surround themselves. When I returned home it was to curtainless windows, bare wooden or linoleum floors, scrubbed tables and stools – not a floral teapot or cake-stand in sight. One would have to be totally zombied not to have made comparisons. I did, and when invited to partake in the Aunt and Uncle scheme, declined.

Towards the end of the year I received a surprise visit from Meg. Apparently I had been forgiven. I was delighted to see her, but not the sullen-looking sailor she brought with her. While we talked in the hall, he shuffled from one foot to another, all the while looking embarrassed and uncomfortable. She wanted to know if I could lend her some money. I told her that the only savings I had were with Jeanie. She pleaded with me to let her send a telegram to Jeanie in my name asking for my Post Office book. I was reluctant to do this because I knew that if I gave my money to Meg I might never get it back. However, Meg seemed desperate so I agreed to her request. She also suggested that she take a pair of my shoes away to have them repaired. Despite knowing they would end up in the pawnshop, I handed them over.

Her spirits revived at the prospect of getting my money soon, she suggested we go into town for a cup of coffee (shades of my visit to the cinema in Inverness). This was too much for her companion, who, unhampered by any of the niceties dictated by good breeding, registered his disapproval by insisting that if she brought me along he would go his own way. Meg held her ground; insisted I came too. This 'gentleman' then turned on his heel, and marched outside and down the driveway towards the main road. Poor Meg!

We watched his departure from a narrow window in the first floor corridor. As his figure moved farther and farther away, Meg's consternation grew more acute. "What will I do, Jound?" she asked, her delicate, sensitive hands trembling as she dabbed away the liquid evidence of her true feelings, "I love him." What could I do? I urged her to go after him. She kissed me gently on the cheek, squeezed my right hand and off she went, her shapely legs flying, much as they had done when she ran through the myrtle at Culantyre.

I watched from the window. My poor, poor Meg; still a dreamer; still very vulnerable! I drew some consolation from the fact that at least I couldn't be twisted round someone's little pinkie like a piece of cotton thread. But my romantic, emotional, delicate Meg was for the moment safe with his arm round her waist – she of the searching soul was temporarily propped up by someone who had none. I never did see my shoes again.

Meg's visit set off a chain of events which led to my being released from Castlemilk, but not before Christmas had come and gone. She re-appeared the following week to see if I had heard from Jeanie. When I told her I had not, she sent a telegram to Culantyre requesting Jeanie to send her my Post Office book by return. Jeanie replied advising Meg she had sent the book in a parcel to me before Christmas. I immediately challenged Matron. She denied receiving any such parcel. I didn't believe her but I couldn't prove it.

A few weeks later the Assistant Matron asked if she could have a word with me in private. In a small room, probably her study, she showed me a wine-coloured Platignum pen and asked if it was mine. I replied, "No." She then handed me a red hard-backed exercise book. I felt my face flush. I knew before I opened it that it was the Latin exercise book I had left behind at Culantyre the previous January. The pen, was mine after all – not only had Jeanie given it to me for my Christmas, it was the same pen that I had used to write the first few pages of a detective story in the exercise book now in my hands. I opened the book. The detective story had been ripped out, but in my handwriting on the inside hardback cover was the following childish poem I had composed at Culantyre –

Amo, amas, Amat
What on earth is that
You stupid fool, go back to school
Don't you know
That's Latin.

Amamus, amatis, amant
Learn Latin I can't
The teacher sits
And glares at me
Tells me I ashamed should be
For being slow at Latin.

Exams are here
And how I fear
In Latin I shall fail.
Results at last.
What's that, I've passed
Hooray, I'm first in Latin.

Despite my anger at having been deprived of my Christmas parcel from Jeanie, I kept control. I was not being handed the contents of a 'lost parcel recently retrieved', for where was Jeanie's letter, and why had I not been informed my Post Office book had come with the pen and exercise book? Rumour had it that the Assistant Matron and Matron had fallen out. Was this one of the side effects? Who knows. That night I wrote to father, whose address I now knew, and asked him to call. When he appeared I told him the whole story and advised him not to approach Matron but to go to John Street, the headquarters of the Corporation as soon as possible. Within days of father registering my complaint, I was on the move again.

No one explained why. However, I really did not mind. This time I had done nothing wrong. I was being moved, I believed, because of someone else's lies, someone else's theft. Furthermore, I felt that no matter where I was going, it could not be more soul-destroying than the place I was leaving.

It was one of the fastest removals I had experienced. Fortunately, apart from my pen and exercise book, I had nothing to pack, and apart from Mrs. McQuater, no one to miss or who would miss me.

10

CHAPTER TEN
Last Lap

I was sent to Clyde Cottage, a small home in Dunoon, which catered for some twenty girls, whose ages ranged from ten to fifteen.

The building was basically an L-shaped bungalow, the main part of which housed four small dormitories, Matron's room, cook's room, and the maid's room. To the left of the sleeping quarters was a beautiful playroom, but it was only opened when we had important visitors. Branching off to the right of the playroom, were the bathroom, kitchen, dining-room, wash-house and store. When we were not playing in the garden or the wash-house the dining-room was used as our playroom.

Our lives were strictly regimented. We rose at seven; made our beds; swept and polished our dormitories, then washed and brushed our teeth before breakfasting at eight. Everyone, regardless of which school she attended, left the premises at eight-thirty. Tea was served at 5 p.m. and by 7.30 p.m. we were all in bed, with the exception of the two oldest girls who were allowed to remain up until half-past eight.

It was those 'big girls' as they were known, who allocated our chores for the week and who supervised the distribution of clean clothing on Sundays.

It did not take me long to realise that the 'big girls' wielded a fair degree of authority and were accorded a status unheard of in any other home I had inhabited. One of the unwritten rules was that we were not supposed "to cheek them." This seemed reasonable enough provided they did not overstep their authority. But alas, it was not long before I found myself challenging that authority.

On my second day there, I asked one of the girls when I could have a bath. She looked flabbergasted. After a great deal of eye-rolling and smirking for the benefit of everyone else in the room, she replied "You're only allowed to have a bath on Sundays," adding as an afterthought, "and the big girls bathe you." It was my turn to be flabbergasted.

I was an old hand at setting the boundaries of my territory and grabbed the opportunity to hammer in the first fence post. I pointedly looked down at my bust, breathed in deeply as I looked round the room and asked, "Which big girls?" The two oldest girls stood up. They said not one word, but I could read the challenge in their eyes. "You'll not be bathing me," I said in my most refined accent. "I bathe myself." "We'll see," said one. The challenge made, Sunday would bring the confrontation.

When Sunday came round I was allocated the chore everyone hated – peeling the potatoes. If this was a punishment, it backfired. I enjoyed peeling potatoes and as the cook, Miss Brown, was always popping in out of the kitchen for a chat, my chore was doubly pleasant. (As it turned out, because everyone else detested potato peeling, I was allowed to keep it as my permanent chore).

At five-thirty, the younger girls began disappearing two by two into the bathroom. It was almost six-thirty when my name was called. Despite an uncomfortable feeling in my stomach, I sauntered into the bathroom as though I hadn't a care in the world. As I had anticipated, the 'big girls' were waiting for me. One was sitting on the edge of the bath, swinging her left leg in an effort to give the impression of composure. The other was fussing nervously over the sink. In order to drain the half-full bath, I bent down to pull out the plug. The girl sitting on the edge of the bath jumped up. "What do you think you're doing?" she demanded shrilly. "Changing the bath water," I replied coolly. My coolness dissipated rapidly, however, when I was informed I was expected to bathe in the grey, tepid water in which, I later discovered, every child younger than I had already bathed – approximately seventeen!

I relinquished my hold on the plug and without looking at either of them, stormed down to Matron's room to demand that she accompany me to the bathroom. When she saw the water I was expected to bathe in, she agreed with my demand that the water be changed. Now I had to win the right to bathe in privacy.

It has been my experience in institutions that there is always an accepted pecking order. In Clyde Cottage it was apparently determined by age. In this particular instance, it was not a pecking order I was prepared to accept. I insisted the 'big girls' leave the bathroom. Matron once again gave way. From that day on I was allowed not only to bathe in clean water but in privacy, but only after the 'big girls' had bathed. This meant my bath water was clean but lukewarm. I never could understand why our baths were not spaced out during the week. It was common knowledge the dining-room boiler took an hour to heat sufficient water for a bath!

Needless to say, I wasn't the most popular person in Clyde Cottage and when the 'big girls' distributed our clean underwear, I was convinced my torn vest and stained, navy flannel knickers were not the result of random selection.

Not wishing to create too much havoc in my first week, I determined to say nothing. Unfortunately, when I discovered I was expected to do P.T at school in my underwear, I was back at Matron's door. In the privacy of her study, I stripped off my knickers and showed her the large white stain in the crotch. I made my position clear. Until I was given stain-free knickers I would not only refuse to do P.T but I would tell the teacher why. I was immediately supplied with a pair of pristine knickers and the following week our complete supply of knickers was replenished.

While I had convinced Matron that I was strong-willed, I had not yet convinced the older girls I could not be tamed. In short, I had to prove myself physically. However, as I normally retaliated to verbal aggression in kind, this proved a little more difficult than they had anticipated. Whether the following incident arose by accident or design I am unable to say.

I was playing on my own in the wash-house when one of the younger girls rushed in and ran behind my back, shouting "Protect me, Helen, protect me." She was immediately followed by one of the older girls who made several ineffectual attempts to hit her. After a few moments, during which I was jostled between them, I told them to take their differences elsewhere. Without warning, the older girl lashed out and hit me squarely on the chin. As I didn't believe the punch was meant for the girl jumping about behind my back, I grabbed my assailant and told her that when I let go she would be well-advised to walk away. When I released my grip she ladled into me, punching indiscriminately with both fists. Now I was angry. She had been warned. Willie had told me that the nearer you stand to a horse, the less injury you will sustain if it kicks you. With this in mind, I stayed close to my attacker and waited until I could throw one good punch. When the opportunity presented itself, I stepped back, let fly and split her ear lobe. I think it was the sight of her blood rather than the pain that forced her to flee in terror to Matron. Matron accepted my version of events and advised my attacker to be more careful in future. I had established my place in the herd and, thank goodness, was never physically challenged again.

Along with everyone over twelve, I attended Dunoon Grammar School, which was actually a comprehensive school. On my first morning there I was asked what school I had attended prior to coming to Dunoon. I replied, "Queenspark Junior Secondary," and was placed in lD, a non-academic stream. About four weeks later, at the end of the last period of the day, my form master asked me to stay behind. When the classroom had emptied, he asked me to translate some Latin and French sentences he had written in an exercise book. After I had finished translating them into English he told me to run off home.

The following morning I was called to the headmaster's study. When I came through his door, Mr. Brown was sitting behind a large, paper-strewn desk. Terrified, I sat in the chair opposite him and waited to hear what I had done wrong. Instead of the anticipated lecture, he asked if I was settling in all right and if I found my class work difficult. I replied "Yes," to the first question and "No," to the second. He shuffled around some papers and then said he had been looking at my class results and they seemed to be unusually high. I sat still, uncomfortably still. What was I supposed to reply? He then asked how I managed to translate the Latin and French, which my form master had given me. When I told him I had been taught languages at Inverness Academy he invited me to tell him all about my schooling since passing the Bursary,

I recounted my time at Inverness Academy, Dalbeattie Senior Secondary, Albert Drive Academy, the primary school in the grounds of Castlemilk, the periods without schooling and finally Queenspark Junior Secondary. A look of disbelief mixed with anger crept momentarily over his face. Without saying another word he picked up the phone and asked to be put through to the Children's Department of Glasgow Corporation.

After he was connected to an official at the other end, I heard him say all the things I had wanted to say about my education but had never had the opportunity to voice, and I was pleased that someone was doing it for me. At the same time I was apprehensive I might, as a result of his telephone call, be moved to another home and I was quite happy in Clyde Cottage. So great was this fear, the only words I can recall verbatim were, "It's not for you to decide what form of schooling a child is capable of undertaking. That is the responsibility of the Education Department." I could have kissed him. When he put the phone down he told me I was to go into lA immediately and urged me to try my best to catch up with the class.

When I returned to Clyde Cottage, I went straight to Matron's office. When she saw me, she visibly paled, but when I told her my good news she seemed genuinely pleased.

A week or two later my gym-slip was replaced with a beautiful pleated skirt. Matron explained this was necessary, as my mature figure looked ridiculous in a gym-slip. Not surprisingly, as I was the only girl in Clyde Cottage who wore a skirt to school, I was looked on with envy and suspicion by the rest of the girls. (I think we all wore skirts to school by the time I left).

As well as the wonderful and stimulating change to my school environment, I received an unexpected bonus. During a visit by a Mr. McLeish, a Children's Officer I had met briefly in Castlemilk, he handed me my 'lost' Post Office Savings Book, for which I had to sign a receipt. After a few minutes of idle chat he asked if I would like to go to dancing lessons. Apparently Matron had told the Corporation that I spent a great deal of time dancing on the lawn or attempting to perform simple acrobatics. I couldn't believe my ears. My education and now dancing lessons. Someone was surely looking after me.

Later that afternoon, when Matron confirmed that I was to be sent to ballet and Highland dancing classes, my happiness was almost painful. I felt as if my chest was about to burst and I longed to run to my secret island at Culantyre to tell the rowan trees how wonderful, how exciting my life was; how once again I was at one with them – growing and flourishing. I felt sure Matron, despite our initial differences, now respected and trusted me. Yes, these were rewards for honesty and hard work. And when one of the girls suggested I was being given special privileges because Matron was afraid of me, I ignored her remarks, put them down to jealousy. You do not give privileges to someone you do not like. Besides, afraid of what? No, these were rewards because she was proud of me.

What my dancing instructress made of my physique, I shudder to think. At 5ft 2 in and weighing almost nine and a half stone, I must have looked an odd figure in the muslin tutu Miss Brown had lovingly made for me. I spent hours practising on the lawn, stretching and pulling my body into the most unnatural positions until my head and back ached. Put into block shoes immediately (a practice that would have been denigrated by any reputable ballet mistress) my toes blistered and bled. In order to prevent this, I bathed my feet every night in methylated spirits until my skin hardened and the bleeding stopped.

My studies, however, did not go as smoothly as my dancing. I was well behind the class in Maths, Science, French and Latin and I had only eight or ten weeks in which to catch up. By the end of the term, I had caught up with the class in everything except Latin. When Mr. Brown suggested I drop Latin and transfer into 2C I was very disappointed. But he had a valid point. If I repeated lA, which I wanted to do, I would have been fifteen by the time I finished the first year. I had to agree, albeit reluctantly, that it made more sense to go into the second year. (Some twenty years later I gained an '0' level Latin after eight months study and I prize that certificate above all others).

When allowed out, most of my first summer at Clyde Cottage was spent wandering about the streets, watching and listening to the tourists who flooded in by the boatload. Package holidays were a rare thing then. In order to cater for the visitors, the numerous theatres put on summer shows and ran talent competitions. Several of our girls entered these competitions and won prizes for singing. If my memory is correct, three of the girls were very talented sopranos. In fact we seemed to have more than the average sprinkling of talent

8. The "three musketeers". Left to right - me, Jeanette and Marabelle.

in Clyde Cottage. The most talented, as far as I was concerned, was Mary, a buxom lass of Irish extraction, who astonished me by her insistence upon wearing not one, but two brassieres! Mary wrote the most beautiful poetry – not doggerel – but sensitive, observant verses. Despite the fact that we had had several verbal clashes, I was a great admirer of Mary. Not only was she a master of the written word, but she could tell such witty stories; make adjectives dance either in rows or around words with such expertise none of us could tell if there was a glimmer of truth in her tales; for Mary had the gift of the blarney. I rather suspect that she was more than capable of pursuing academic studies, but somehow or other, like many of the children, her education came very low down in the list of priorities the Corporation deemed essential for her care. How short-sighted can one be.

Amongst the twenty or so children in Clyde Cottage, two stick out in my memory. One was a refined, delicate child of about ten. Her responses, both physical and mental, were so slow you could have been forgiven for mistaking her for a dullard, but I always suspected her slowness was due to some deep trauma. I felt very protective towards her and spent a great deal of time brushing her hair in a futile attempt to rid her of the dandruff that plagued her. At first I also tried to teach her to read and write, but when I realised she didn't want to learn, I stopped. I had made this mistake at Eversley when my attempts to instil my standards into younger children had really been a form of bullying, and that was something I never wanted to do again.

The other child scarred by some unknown trauma was a fleeting resident. She was about seven when she arrived in our midst. We were asked to be especially kind to her. But the little girl refused to speak, limiting her responses to our attentions to a simple "Yes," or "No." Because of her mental fragility, she was put in my dormitory in order that we could keep an eye on her. During her first night with us, a strange, rhythmical thumping awakened me. Thinking that there were burglars in the room, I jumped from my bed and switched on the light, only to discover that the newcomer was lying on her back, her eyes staring vacantly into space as she banged her head up and down on her pillow. I had seen distressed children rocking backwards and forwards but I had never seen this. In the morning I reported her strange behaviour to Matron. Unfortunately, despite our concerned attentions, after a few days she refused to say a single word. We were all surprised, therefore, when one afternoon she suddenly burst into song. One after another poured from her previously silent throat. As she went through her repertoire, one of the girls, who knew every 'pop' song, commented that none of the songs she sang had come out in the last two years. We assumed that something horrible had happened to her two years ago; something which, apart from her singing, had rendered her mute.

How long this unfortunate child stayed with us, I do not recollect, but for a few days after she had gone I found a phrase from one of Lord Byron's poems flitting into my mind on the most odd occasions – "We who have grown old in deeds, not years." And the fear and insecurity I had felt in Castlemilk returned to settle briefly, like a dark, grey cloud, over my otherwise happy life. My short acquaintance with this little girl merely confirmed my suspicion that the only predator man has to fear is man.

Within a few days of the new school year starting, I made friends with two of my classmates – Marabelle Douglas and Jeanette Boyd. Marabelle had an irrepressible sense of humour and eyes that sparkled all day long. Even more fascinating, when she laughed, those sparkling eyes spouted tears. Jeanette was quieter, but she had a ready wit and her dry observations on people and their behaviour, invariably left me doubled up with laughter

What these two lively girls saw in me, I do not know. Compared to them, I had few anecdotes to swap, and although I certainly had much more freedom than I had enjoyed at Castlemilk, I still could not come and go as I pleased. We did, however, manage to persuade Matron to let me out for bicycle trips on Saturday afternoons. Marabelle borrowed a bicycle from one of her friends and on sunny days we would cycle into the countryside and picnic beside little-frequented streams. Mind you, had Matron known my bicycle had no brakes I doubt very much if she would have let me go. Those were marvellous days - days of freedom from institutions and the ever-watchful eyes of others. Days when together we screamed at the pure joy of being young and energetic. We spent most of our time speaking to each other in a nonsense language and laughing hysterically over absolutely nothing at all. Even in the classroom we communicated as if by telepathy – little wonder we were known as 'The Three Musketeers' – we were inseparable.

Another classmate who brought endless hours of pleasure into my life was a slim, red-haired girl called Gillian McDiarmid. Gillian had an interest in ballet and loaned me expensive books to drool over. She also cut out photographs of ballet dancers from magazines and newspapers and gave them to me to keep. Through her I became the proud possessor of a large coloured photograph of Margot Fonteyn in Spectre de la Rose. I pasted this beautiful picture on to a piece of cardboard and it became my most treasured possession. I spent hours looking at that photograph. Miss Fonteyn's head, shoulders, arms and legs were positioned in one flowing movement and yet she had been standing still when the photograph had been taken.

Although I was at ease with the girls in my class, the boys I left strictly alone, or perhaps, more truthfully, they left me alone. At fourteen-and-a-half, although shafts of desire to be noticed were surfacing, I was still a total innocent as far as boys were concerned. I think the problem arose from the fact that I probably presented an insurmountable challenge in that I did not understand the finer nuances of flirting. Invariably when approaches were made, my blank, unresponsive face would force my admirer to back off. How I managed to leave school so ignorant about boys completely mystifies me. The older girls must have discussed them at some time.

When Christmas came round, I got a handbag from Jeanie and a jar of Pond's Cold Cream and a lipstick from the church. I remember being quite surprised at receiving such a worldly present from a religious organisation.

For my first official school dance, Matron loaned me a green crepe dress and I borrowed a pair of high heels from one of the older girls. Oh, the excitement when I danced with two of my teachers - all grown up on the outside but a child still occupying the inside. Funny how it's not the overall picture you remember. It's bits, colours, and smells. For me it was mainly the lipstick – its smell, its taste and the oily smoothness it gave to my lips.

Under the assumption that I would leave school at the Easter term, I had asked if I might go and live with Mrs. McQuater in Glasgow. However, when the Easter holidays came and went and I was still attending school, it seemed probable that I might be allowed to continue my education, for it was most unusual to remain in a home beyond working age.

At the end of the summer term, I was pleased, but not ecstatic with my results. I think I was amongst the first three in every subject except music, for which I got the appallingly low mark of 16%. As I am tone deaf, I knew my mark would be low, but when I learned that I had missed the overall class prize by eleven marks I felt cheated.

During the summer holidays we were invited to exchange places with children from another home, Gryffe Castle in Renfrewshire. Like the rest of the girls, I spent several days trekking up and down the main street searching for luxuries to buy for this, my first holiday. In the end, as I was saving up to go to Glasgow for a day with Marabelle and Jeanette, I limited my purchases to a cake of Lux toilet soap and a pink satin handkerchief trimmed with lace.

Gryffe Castle, like Castlemilk, was a very large institution set in beautiful wooded grounds. Unlike Castlemilk, however, the interior was light and airy. The ground floor dormitories had beautiful French windows, which overlooked the landscaped garden and the dining-room not only boasted small tables, but on each there was a water decanter and four tumblers – an unheard of luxury. Further, not only was the delicious food served up in quantities sufficient to

9. Gryffe Castle - now private flats.

satiate my appetite, but we also had a choice of menu! It was like being in an upmarket holiday camp.

Matron, a married lady in her late thirties or early forties, took a great pride in being fit and supple and my acrobatic displays pleased her so much that before three days had passed she mentioned she would like me to pay a return visit. (Whether this was to be with the second group from Clyde Cottage or on my own, I cannot remember).

During my week at Gryffe Castle, I did not, as some of the other girls did, pair off with any of the boys. I much preferred to spend my time playing netball, walking down leafy lanes to the small village shop to buy nougat, or sticking close to a softly spoken lady whose job it was to entertain us. I had never met anyone so refined or intelligent working in homes before. She fascinated me.

I never did get to spend a second week at Gryffe Castle. The day before our group was due to return home, sex reared its ugly head. I was in the dormitory writing a letter to Jeanie when Matron entered in an agitated state and announced that she was going to search our lockers and cases. During her search I learned that she was looking for love-letters. This was the first I had heard of such 'heinous' activity. I couldn't understand what all the fuss was about.

When Matron reached my bed I allowed her to search both my locker and my case. After satisfying herself that they held no incriminating evidence, she asked me to hand over my handbag, which I had been holding on to. It was the wrong move. Unlike Matron at Clyde Cottage, she was unfamiliar with my ideas of dignity. I had felt slightly annoyed at her intrusion into my privacy when she had searched my locker and case. At the same time, I considered those to be the property of Glasgow Corporation and whether I liked it or not, that she had a right to look through them. My handbag, however, the one Jeanie had sent me, I considered to be my private property and no one was going to rummage through it.

I refused to hand it over. When she repeated her request, I pointed out that it contained nothing of interest to her; it belonged to me and if she insisted upon searching it I was prepared to protect my property with any means at my disposal. Everyone in the dormitory who came from Clyde Cottage froze. They knew I had certain idiosyncrasies about my personal possessions and they knew I meant what I said. Did Matron know?

We stared into each other's eyes for what seemed an uncomfortably long time. I felt trapped. If she made to take it from me I would have to back up my threat. Threats had always worked before, always ensured no one intruded into what I defined as my territory. But this was not a woman to be intimidated by threats. I knew it. She knew it. She gave way, not out of fear but respect. She knew that in the end she had the upper hand, but despite the audience, she was big enough to back away and leave me with my 'dignity'. Not only a woman with superb physical strength, but a woman with an inner perception I had never met before.

When we returned to Clyde Cottage, the rumpus over the love-letters continued. Matron interviewed everyone. My assertion that I had nothing to do with the boys was readily accepted but the rest of the girls still had to endure an interrogation over the colour of the underskirts they had worn at Gryffe Castle! (Matron later confided in me that the Gryffe Castle Matron had asked me back for a further week because she not only admired my physical prowess, but my 'spunk' – unfortunately the rumpus put paid to a return visit).

When I recounted the handbag incident to Matron, she seemed pleased that someone else had had to cope, albeit temporarily, with my convoluted idea of what did or did not constitute an infringement of my 'rights'.

When I returned to school at the end of August and entered 3C I became a prefect and was elected Class Captain and Captain of the netball team. Alas, I had only been back at school a month or two when whatever was planned for my future was torn to shreds by me.

I was standing on one of the swings on the lawn when one of the girls decided to whisper her eavesdropping in my ears. Apparently, on some indeterminate occasion, she had heard Matron discussing my future with a representative of the Corporation who wanted her to keep me at Clyde Cottage until I sat my Highers. According to my informant, she had indicated she was none too happy about this as I was troublesome and very difficult to handle.

When I heard the word 'troublesome' my arms went limp and I slumped down on to the seat of the swing. My informant, realising it would have been more prudent if she had kept her eavesdropping to herself, ran off and left me to digest this unwanted piece of information. I felt betrayed. How could Matron say such a thing – she who had sent me to my dancing lessons, allowed me to go out for bicycle runs and had told me, with what I thought was pride, that I was capable of succeeding in any field. I couldn't understand it. I obeyed all the rules. Anger is a pure feeling which brings with it justification for retaliation. Hurt brings out the same outward reactions but the justification for them is less clearly defined.

I recalled the words of the girl who had told me Matron only gave me special privileges because she was afraid of me. At the time I had dismissed her allegations as ludicrous. I had assumed she meant physically afraid. Now I began to wonder if perhaps she had meant something else. In view of what I had just heard, it seemed I had not been given my special privileges because Matron had recognised my talents, or because I had won her respect. I had been given them as a bribe to keep me from taking my observations outside. The disparity between Matron's actions and her opinion of me filled me with dismay. Whatever else I was, I was no 'toady'. Neither my loyalty nor my integrity was for sale. I had obviously failed to win her respect and she wanted rid of me.

Minutes after I had reached this conclusion, Matron passed me on her way to the wash-house. As she passed, I said in a loud, carrying voice, "Some people are two-faced." She visibly paled but walked on. Ten minutes later I was called to her study and asked to explain myself. I told her that her conversation about my future had been relayed to me and I could not equate her words with her actions. She reminded me of the trouble I had caused over bathing in clean water and wearing clean knickers. I replied that I thought my behaviour was justified. She did not respond, but now insisted I withdraw my statement in front of the other girls. I explained that, while I regretted voicing my opinion, to withdraw it publicly or privately would mean I no longer held that opinion, and as far as I was concerned, that would be a lie. She then informed me that unless I withdrew my remark publicly I would be returned to Glasgow forthwith.

I was now faced with a dilemma. I had spent the past three years trying to undo the lies I had told at Dalbeattie and, in an attempt to regain my reputation, now fiercely protected my integrity. I had also spent a considerable part of those three years frustrated because I was not receiving the education to which

I believed I was entitled. On the surface it was a choice between my education and my 'honour'. But it was more than that. Matron obviously wanted rid of me. I refused to withdraw my remark. Two days later I was removed from school.

Aged fifteen and a half and with only one full year of secondary education behind me, namely the second year, I left for Glasgow. I took with me an impossibly rigid code of behaviour, a deep-rooted distrust of authority, a wealth of experiences and observations, an almost childlike innocence about the outside world, a zest and enthusiasm for life and hard work, and, most important, my eternal optimism. I would succeed. Good things would happen to me. With those intangibles I took a cardboard case containing a half-used jar of Pond's Cold cream, an almost unused lipstick, a pink satin handkerchief, a photograph of Margot Fonteyn, a navy handbag, nine shillings and the clothes I was wearing - all my worldly possessions.

I had fought a relentless enemy,
Whose armour was his stealth,
Oh, had I known, what I now know,
That enemy was myself.

11

CHAPTER ELEVEN
Journey's End

10. Burnbank Gardens where my first hostel stood. The Gardens are now partially demolished

As I sped towards my new life, I prayed I would now be free of matrons and restrictive regulations. Meanwhile, I had a few unknowns to ponder. Would I be given pocket money to tide me over until I found employment; what sort of job could I get without any qualifications; would I be given a room of my own; had father been told of my move and would I be allowed to visit him? Uppermost in my mind, however, was whether or not my new resting-place had radiators on which I could dry my one and only pair of pants.

I entered my new world, the one for those such as me, the flotsam and jetsam of domestic upheaval and war, through the door of a hostel in Burnbank Gardens, Maryhill, Glasgow, only to discover I had merely traded in my Clyde Cottage dormitory for a smaller but equally spartan one.

After being introduced to Matron and her Assistant, Miss Brown, I was left in the care of Mary, a small, middle-aged lady plagued by asthma and eczema. Unable to work, she augmented whatever small income she had by doing little jobs around the hostel for Matron, Miss Brown or the part-time cook, Miss Johnstone. On this occasion she had been delegated to take me on a tour of the building.

We started in the basement, which housed a large kitchen, containing an exceptionally long table, numerous cupboards and a range upon which stood a gigantic kettle that was kept permanently 'just off the boil'. Abutting on to the kitchen was a formal, rarely used dining-room, the table, chairs and floor of which were polished to perfection. Finally, adjacent to the dining-room, lay the coal cellar and wash-house, the latter being equipped with two deep sinks, a clothes pulley (presently draped with a variety of clothes), an ironing board and iron.

The ground floor was entered through a beautiful, stained glass door, which led into a wide hall. To the immediate right lay the largest living-room I had ever seen,which, like the dining-room, was obviously rarely used. Next to this magnificent, but genteelly shabby room, were the staff offices and toilet.

The first floor was entirely given over to Matron, her daughter and Miss Brown. Although not permitted to view this floor on my supervised tour, I later observed that it was comfortably furnished and carpeted.

My tour completed, Mary and I returned to the basement kitchen where she ran through the house rules. It transpired that my life would be less regulated than hitherto, but more regulated than I had anticipated.

We breakfasted at 8 a.m. except on Sundays, when we ate an hour later. Curfew was at 10 p.m., except on Saturdays, when it was extended to accommodate the late film at the Gem, a small cinema in Great Western Road. On Sundays, morning church service, and evening hymn singing in Matron's lounge, were obligatory. Permission had to be sought if we wished to leave the hostel, even if only for five minutes, and our destination and length of absence conveyed to Matron.

Finally, there was 'duty week'. Everyone, except the staff, had to take their turn at rising at 6 a.m. to set the table, light the kitchen range, make porridge, boil the kettle and toast numerous slices of bread in front of the range – no such thing as a toaster here. We also had to be on duty in the evening to prepare trays of tea and biscuits for Matron, Miss Brown and their guests, many of whom were local police officers.

Does the leopard change his spots? Upon hearing of the evening duty, I felt the hairs on the back of my neck rising as if they were being tugged towards the heavens by an invisible magnet. I was not a maid. Why could the staff not make their own tea? In their defence, however, Matron's daughter occasionally collected the set tray from the kitchen.

During her brief forays into our domain, I have to admit to feeling envious of this twelve or thirteen year old girl. Apart from having a mother and living in comfortable surroundings, she was pretty, self-assured and did not have to cope with the tensions and noise of communal living. But of all the privileges she enjoyed, I was most envious of her education. I believe she attended a fee-paying school. She certainly wore a beautiful school uniform and was learning all the subjects I had forfeited by running away from the Camerons and by subsequently challenging the Matron at Clyde Cottage.

Once, after I confessed I knew a little Latin, she handed me the text book The Approach to Latin, First Part, and asked me to translate a few sentences. I think she was genuinely surprised when I completed her test. But never again was I given the opportunity to display my limited knowledge of that ancient language.

My first evening in the hostel was a revelation in socio-economics. When the girls gathered round the table for the evening meal, the conversation, for my enlightenment, turned to jobs and salaries. Three of the girls worked in a factory, two in a department store, one in an office, one in a wool shop and one, in her mid to late twenties, worked as a chemist in Boots.

The factory girls worked a five-day week for approximately £4; the girls in the department store worked a five-and-a-half-day week for £2.10s and the office girl worked a five-day week for £2.10s. I never did learn what the qualified chemist earned. An enigma, older and wiser than the rest, she kept her earnings and her background to herself.

From the above information I was able to deduce that unqualified employees earn less if they work in a warm, comfortable environment than they do working on a factory floor. As I did not want to work in a factory, and I felt more than capable of working in a shop, it was highly likely that my salary would barely cover my living expenses – the hostel charged £1.10s per week for board and lodgings. It looked as if my aim to buy my first home at the age of twenty-one was over-optimistic.

Later that evening a more urgent problem occupied my mind – my ablutions. When I confided in Mary that I had neither flannel, soap or towel with which to wash and dry myself, she promptly led me into the wash-house, pulled two dishcloths from the pulley, grabbed a tablet of washing soap from one of the sinks and sliced it in two before handing me one half, plus the two dishcloths. "There," she said triumphantly, "Soap, one flannel and one towel." My problem was temporarily solved.

The following morning I was called to Matron's study and informed that during the next six weeks she would assess me for what type of work she thought I would be suitable. At the end of that period she would also assess whether I was trustworthy enough to be allowed to visit father on my own. In the meantime, I would receive a weekly allowance of 2/6d. During this period I would only be allowed out of the hostel in the company of one of the other girls.

When I returned to the quiet of my dormitory, the surge of excitement I had felt at the thought of visiting father was replaced with a niggling resentment. Why should someone who did not know me and who, as far as I was aware, was neither a careers mistress or psychologist, assess my work suitability?

I consoled myself with the thought that in another six weeks I would be working and at least have some control over my life. Meanwhile, I would put up, shut up, listen and learn, and I certainly had a lot to learn. In my day, children brought up in care were shielded from a lot of information – no wireless, no newspapers, few visitors and no adult conversation overheard at the dinner table. I may have been literate, numerate and capable of verbally holding my own, but street wise I was not.

Towards noon, our weekly rations were distributed in the kitchen – 4 oz of margarine, 2 oz of butter (on alternate weeks this was raised to 4 oz) and 1 lb of sugar.

In the afternoon, Mary accompanied me to shop for the necessities, amongst which were, one bar of soap, two facecloths (one to be used as a towel), a toothbrush, a tin of Gibb's pink toothpaste and two pairs of white cotton pants. These purchases used up the weekly pocket money I had received from Matron and a fair portion of the savings I had brought with me. As I was not permitted to accompany the rest of the girls on their customary Saturday night visit to the Gem cinema , in case I ran away, I was left to my own devices in the basement kitchen.

All was quiet. All was tranquil. I settled in front of the roaring range fire, toasted numerous slices of bread, which I spread liberally with the communal lard (being careful to preserve my rations of margarine and butter) and luxuriated in the warmth and unaccustomed privacy. Round about 8 p.m. the silence was penetrated by music coming from the dance hall next door. Unfamiliar with the popular tunes of the day, but mesmerised by the rhythm, I rose from my chair and threw myself from one end of the room to the other, lost in the exhilaration of moving my body in time to the music.

The following morning, I awoke to the unfamiliar smell of bacon and eggs being cooked by Rose, one of the factory workers. Try as I might, I cannot remember having eaten a fried or boiled egg the whole of my time in the homes. I can only presume these were too difficult to cook for large numbers of children and they were either used up in scrambled eggs, which I do not recall, or in baking, which certainly never reached us.

After breakfast, there was much coming and going as we all prepared for church; all that is except Matron, her daughter and Rose, who remained behind to cook lunch - the part-time cook did not work on Sundays. We left in a group, each wearing a hat and gloves, and, as if to advertise our godliness, clutching large bibles. In order that I should conform, Mary loaned me a pair of white, cotton gloves and a white, felt hat trimmed with netting. As I was wearing my heavy, flat shoes and ankle socks, the addition of the felt hat and white gloves made me feel and look ludicrous.

As we filed towards our pew, our progress being followed by many pairs of curious eyes, the office girl, Cathy, obviously in her element at so much attention, smiled broadly at anyone who caught her eye. During the hymn singing, which took place standing up, I saw several males casting covetous glances in her direction. That men should find her attractive was not surprising; that lustful looks were darting across the floor of God's house I found disturbing.

By the time we returned home, Rose had prepared a Sunday lunch of home-made soup, roast beef, roast potatoes, Yorkshire puddings, carrots, peas and a beautiful fruit-laden trifle. We were joined at the table by the staff – shades of the Camerons. What was it about religious people, or people who claimed to be religious, that they seemed to think they were fulfilling their Christian duty by eating separately throughout the week and only dining with their charges on the Sabbath?

After lunch I retired to my dormitory to ruminate about my present and my future. It was not long, however, before Cathy popped her head round the door and asked if I would like to accompany her for a walk in Kelvingrove Park. Would I indeed? I practically flew off my bed and, after checking it was all right with Matron, trotted excitedly behind Cathy to inspect my new environs and familiarise myself with my home town.

Despite the weak September sun, the park was busy. Several middle-aged couples sat on the benches lining the pathways and young men lay sprawled out on the grass, smoking, talking and laughing. As we approached the latter, they let out long, loud wolf-whistles – for Cathy, not for me. Next to the ultra-feminine Cathy I cut a somewhat pathetic figure with my straight hair, lack of make-up and ill-fitting coat, not to mention the heavy, flat shoes and ankle socks. Cathy, on the other hand, was dressed in a fitting floral dress, which, despite her white cardigan, showed off her figure to perfection. Carefully applied make-up enhanced her good looks and her high heels and glass nylons emphasised her slim and perfectly turned ankles.

Although ignored by the young men, I experienced a vicarious thrill when they whistled at Cathy. I found her company exciting. She was so bubbly and optimistic. No-one had destroyed her personality or squashed her into the ground.

She did not strike me as an intellectual, but she had that other quality necessary for survival – she knew her strengths and how to use them. She was certainly street wise. This may well have been due to the fact she had not spent most of her life in care. Allegedly, she ended up in care after her mother re-married and there was not enough room in their small flat for his children as well as her mother's. This meant she was separated, not only from her mother, but her siblings.

Cathy left the hostel before I did. I hope she made it, because during our short sojourn together she brought hope, laughter and a little glamour into my humdrum life.

When my six-week probationary period was over, Miss Brown took me to a warehouse which supplied the Corporation's children with clothing. I was kitted out with a new outfit, lisle stockings and two bath towels. The following day she accompanied me to one of the first self-service grocery stores in Glasgow for a job interview.

A small, balding, bespectacled man interviewed me in the back shop. When I sailed through the arithmetic test he looked disappointed. Only when I overheard his whispered conversation with Miss Brown did I learn why. The last girl they had employed from the hostel had been caught stealing from the till. When I heard that I blushed till my face nipped with pain and wished I could melt into the floorboards. Miss Brown, however, must have reassured him I was of a different calibre, because I was offered the job and told to report at 8.30 a..m. on the following Monday.

On the return journey to the hostel, I was quieter than usual, concerned that in my first job I would forever be under suspicion, and my every move scrutinised. My new world was letting me down, burdening me with the guilt of someone I had never met. After tea, however, as I sat doodling with figures on numerous scraps of paper, my spirits lifted. I was convinced that in the not too distant future I would be able to buy make-up, nylons and the much-coveted high heels. What I would not be buying, however, were the beautiful, satin, lace-trimmed pants that Cathy wore. I reasoned, as no one would be seeing them, they were a luxury I could do without.

The following Monday, eager to start my working life, I arrived fifteen minutes before opening time, only to be left kicking my heels until the keyholder arrived. Once inside, I was introduced to the staff and then handed two white, starched overalls and two caps. These, I was informed, were to last me all week. Uniform donned, I started my new job by stacking cans in neat horizontal and vertical lines and shuffling packets about until they were lined up like soldiers on parade.

This boring, soul-destroying work was made even less agreeable by the fact we were not allowed to talk to each other. We were, however, allowed two ten-minute tea breaks, which were taken in the back shop where we were allowed to converse. We had to sip our tea perched on top of large wooden crates. I said very little during our breaks but listened intently to tales of 'normal living' by 'normal' people.

On Friday I received my first pay packet - the magical brown envelope that held the key to my future. When I opened it, I was dismayed to discover that, after paying for the laundering of my overalls and caps, plus my National Insurance stamp, my weekly pay of £2 had been whittled down to 32/7d. As my lodgings cost 30/-d this meant, that after working from 8.30 a.m. to 5.30 p.m. Monday to Saturday, with Tuesday afternoon off, my total remuneration was 2/7d, exactly one penny more than my pocket money. I calculated that, provided I saved every penny I earned, it would take me twenty weeks to buy a pair of high heels, six weeks to buy either a pair of nylons or a biro, and three weeks to buy a cheap, sleeveless T-shirt.

Despairing of ever being able to save up anything, I joined the girls for their Saturday trip to the cinema and blew all my pay on a cinema seat, a quarter of pineapple chunks, a chocolate ice cream, 2 chocolate snowballs and a bottle of lemonade. This left me with one penny.

It did not take me long to realise that such profligacy, if it did not quite leave me penniless, would not bring me anywhere near to my dream of being a householder at twenty-one. I therefore stopped going to the cinema and scoffing pineapple chunks, and bought 2/6d saving stamps instead.

As the weeks passed, my working conditions improved. I was put behind the grocery counter where I was tutored in the art of weighing rationed sugar and butter (in brown bags or paper), with an accuracy which brought the needle of the scales just to, but not on, the required weight. I was shown how to intersperse slices of inferior bacon between rashers of fresher, leaner cuts and, colour permitting, to substitute non-rationed duck eggs with the preferred rationed hens' eggs.

Was someone on the fiddle, or did these deceits merely cover stock shortages due to spillage, damage or theft? I did not know. I kept quiet and did what I was told, but along the way perfected a little scam of my own. Once a week, by poking my finger into a luscious cream tart, I was able to buy it at the reduced price of one penny.

I reached the pinnacle of success at work when I was allowed to ring up customers' purchases on the till. This job had several advantages, amongst which was the joy of being able to talk to the customers and to discreetly sell them my sugar and butter rations.

I was learning. Innocence was being eroded. However, in view of my meagre earnings, I did not look upon these activities as criminal. I also augmented my salary by pushing cream sponge cakes on to reluctant buyers on Saturday afternoons. The manager rewarded whoever sold the most with a shilling. My need indubitably being the greatest, and gifted with the blarney, I invariably won this contest. By these means I more than doubled my disposable income but I still saved my 2/6d weekly before spending the remainder.

Apart from learning how to stack cans neatly, wrap and weigh provisions and run up purchases on the till, I was learning other things during my introduction to the way of the outside world. I learned that poorly paid staff resort to helping themselves in kind and I avoided entering the back shop when 'a fair distribution of wealth' took place. It was a co-ordinated exercise. At a pre-determined time, the window of the back shop was flung open and a hail of tins, mainly scarce commodities like salmon and fruit, was thrown into the arms of a waiting accomplice, who sold them on the black market.

Along with my silence on the disappearing tins, I also feigned ignorance when I spotted some of the girls ringing up underpriced goods for members of the staff. My conscience was not troubled by my silence. In my opinion, we were all grossly underpaid. I did not join in these activities because I was good, but rather because I was terrified of being caught.

By the end of my second week, my temporary position was classified as permanent. I cannot say this change in my work status made me whoop for joy, but my next meeting with Matron did. She had decided I could now be trusted to visit father. After handing me an envelope upon which she had written his latest address, she advised me to write and let him know when I would visit him.

On that memorable Sunday, the day of my first visit to father, I could hardly keep still for excitement. I wore my new dress and lisle stockings and, after lunch, flew out of the hostel, half-running, half-skipping towards one of the few links with my past.

When I turned into father's street, the first thing I noticed was the neglected state of the small, front gardens. Few of them had a recognisable lawn, shrub or flower. Many of the windows looked dirty and the curtains were, on the whole, cheap and ill fitting. Alarm bells started ringing.

When I entered the litter-strewn close, I sent up a silent prayer, "Please God, please don't let Dad live like mother." I knocked hesitantly on his door. Above the noise of my pounding heart I heard muffled footsteps, the sound of several keys being turned and locks being unbolted, then he was there – my Dad. He stared at me for a few seconds, cocked his head to the side and said, "Oh, it's you pet. Come on in."

I followed him through the tiny hall, which separated his room from that of his elderly, mainly absent landlady. The memory of mother's living conditions still alive in my mind, I was half-prepared for what met my eyes; nonetheless, years of fantasising were lain waste in seconds, crushed mercilessly beneath the reality which lay before me.

The disintegrating wallpaper was tacked to the wall, its original pattern almost indistinguishable under a patina of cigarette smoke deposits. A rickety table stood to the left of the range which took up most of the right-hand wall. It was strewn with several well-thumbed racing papers, an assortment of chipped mugs and plates and a few pieces of old, mismatched cutlery.

In front of the window, two dining-room chairs supported a wooden rod from which dangled several hangers festooned with damp, bleach-smelling shirts. An old-fashioned dresser, with one door hanging off its hinges, stood opposite the range. In front of it were two brown Rexine-covered armchairs draped with several old jackets and trousers. Directly opposite the window, the bed recess was half-hidden behind a filthy, ragged curtain that was held up by a piece of string. The bed linen did not bear investigation. Neither of the two pillows was covered. I could barely make out the striped black and white ticking beneath the grease that covered them.

I was flabbergasted. Father, like mother, lived in slum-like conditions. Like her, he made no effort to keep his room tidy and clean. It was not what I had hoped for. He had always arrived on his visits looking very smart in his white, starched shirts and highly polished boots. It had never occurred to me that his room would not be clean and tidy. I had one consolation, however, there were no strangers lying in the bed recess.

I watched as father busied himself over the range, heating up a pot of home-made soup and frying a 'wee'chop'. He seemed perfectly relaxed and unaware of my discomfort. When he caught me looking at the clothes hanging between the wooden chairs, he explained apologetically, "The folk round here would have the shirt off your back, let alone the washing line, so I dry them where I can keep my eye on them." I nodded in acknowledgement of his canniness, but wondered whether the drying of wet clothes in such a small room might not be the reason why the wallpaper was peeling away from the wall.

He explained later that he would have liked to paper the room, but he was terrified his landlady would either put up the rent or turf him out for a new tenant, who would be willing to pay more for the room. It was this fear which also led him to keep his landlady's bills as low as possible, which he did by sitting in his room till it was almost dark before switching on the only electric bulb in the room! What I didn't know at the time, however, was that he could have afforded to rent a room and kitchen and put on as many lights as he wished, but he preferred to spend all his disposable income on gambling and boozing. Poor Dad!

When we had finished our meal, which was surprisingly well-cooked, I suggested we go for a walk in Kelvingrove Park which was only minutes away from his flat, but he declined; said he was too busy. He then retrieved a pair of black boots from beneath his bed and with nothing more than a razor, hammer and nails, set about repairing the worn soles and heels. His hands, rough and covered with bulging, tortuous veins, seemed to merge with the leather as he deftly whittled and shaped it to fit his boots. As he concentrated on his task, his eyes glowing with a strange, contented light, I felt proud of his skill. Slum or not, my Dad was a craftsman.

One of the imponderables about my Dad was his attention to detail when it came to his boots (he always wore boots), his starched shirts and his handwriting. He wrote the most beautiful copperplate I have ever seen.

When the hands of the clock reached four, I sensed he had had enough of my presence and rose to leave. As I neared the door, he scooped loose change from the mantelpiece and thrust it into my right hand. I placed the coins in my purse, kissed him shyly on the cheek and, after promising to return at the same time the following week, I was off into the sunshine, caught betwixt and between emotions I could not pigeon-hole, knowing only that I was glad to be out in the fresh air.

After returning to the hostel I ran a hot bath, liberally laced it with dettol, immersed myself in the milky-white liquid and tried to soak away a feeling of disappointment and a vague fear about my future. It was abundantly clear Dad would never agree to share a flat with me - something I had dreamed about. He had chosen his way of life and it was set in concrete. Poor Meg must have been forced to the same conclusion when she had returned from Inverness. Obviously, I would find no help here. I would have to go it alone.

This situation may have accounted for the fact that while I visited father every Sunday, I never saw Meg there. But why I rarely saw her whilst in the

Glasgow hostels, remains a mystery to me. Whatever the reason, I did not find this lack of communication strange or upsetting. She did visit me on one occasion that I can recall, advising me she was married and expecting a baby. I think I was about sixteen at the time. She was, I believe, now living with her mother-in-law in Cranhill, a housing estate on the outskirts of Glasgow.

When I visited her there I found her demeanour similar to that when I had visited her so many years ago at our aunt's – ill at ease and submissive. My lost Meg, gifted with a very high IQ, but presumably without the other qualities necessary for survival, was doomed to spend her short life having to hide her intelligence. It's an incontrovertible fact that some sections of the working class, especially when in the majority, will bully you if they think you are a 'smart ass'. Without a support system to take an interest in her, her IQ remained constant, but her self-esteem plummeted.

As the weeks passed, I learned something new each day in my workplace; the most illuminating of which was that drinking and gambling were not vices limited to my father, but were also to be found amongst the families of my work colleagues.

As I ingested and analysed each new piece of information, I realised that there was a difference between many of my colleagues and me. At first I could not identify it, then one day as I sat on an empty orange box in the back shop it struck me with a clarity I could not ignore. Among my work colleagues there seemed to be a kind of poverty I had never known; an insidious self-perpetuating poverty of soul.

It seemed to me that their main goal in life was to marry young and reproduce. They never talked about their future in terms of improving their lot in life. Had they been brainwashed into accepting it as unchangeable? Was I over-optimistic about my future? Had destiny also selected me to spend the rest of my life working for a low wage? By refusing to apologise to Matron in Clyde Cottage, had I cut off my nose to spite my face? These were questions I did not want to answer.

Whilst these ruminations swirled round, undefined, haphazard in their crystallisation, I moved slowly along my path of learning. On Tuesday afternoons, now that I was permitted out on my own, I roamed round the suburbs, a Peeping Tom in ankle socks, glancing discreetly over hedges and through open windows and doors into numerous bungalows and villas. I loved when the lengthening nights let me see into well-lit homes and the tableaux before me made me more determined than ever to own my own house by the time I was twenty-one.

Despite my 'house-shopping', however, I slowly became aware that those suburban streets and avenues held slivers of life, which, when pieced together, gave me a strange feeling of sadness and loss. Not prepared to face that loss – the loss of a normal childhood – I turned my back on suburbia, and limited my roaming to window-shopping in Sauchiehall Street.

Some time in spring, one of my friends from Clyde Cottage, Christine, returned to Glasgow and was placed as a domestic with a family in Clarkston, one of Glasgow's more affluent suburbs. The only reason we met up again was because her younger sister lived in the Maryhill hostel.

When I learned that she was left with £2 per week all found compared to my net 2/7d, I realised I was in the wrong job and informed Matron I intended to seek work in domestic service. This caused great consternation both at Glasgow Corporation's headquarters and the hostel. It seemed they looked upon me as 'a wrong un' who needed to be held in check. Rather than see me go, they offered to send me to commercial college! So much for Matron's six-week assessment.

This was an amazing piece of news, but even more amazing was the fact I was to be given 5/-d weekly pocket money. When I blurted out that this was almost twice my disposable income from my employment, a bemused Matron asked how I managed to buy my towels. My response, " The Corporation gave me two when I started work," left her completely bewildered, not least because there was one tied round the kitchen door handles to muffle the sound of the door closing. As I had never menstruated, I had no idea what it was for! I was referred immediately to the local doctor who gave me medicine to remedy my condition. It worked, but every month thereafter I endured the most appalling pains during my very light two-day cycle.

I began my secretarial studies in September, 1953, at The Glasgow and West of Scotland Commercial College in Pitt Street. This was my chance to improve my lot, and I had no intention of throwing it away. Whilst my 5/-d a week pocket money was riches to me, when it came to extra curricular activities, I could not afford to socialise with the other girls in the evening, which deprived me of some of the fun of attending college. Instead, I spent my time practising shorthand in the large lounge on the first floor of the hostel. It may have been cold, but it was quiet, It was also a great room in which to do physical exercises.

During the early months of my attendance at college, Christine and I would meet up on Saturdays and spend our time either walking or going to the cinema. One day we popped into a shoemaker's in Maryhill Road and were chatted up by the two young lads behind the counter. We arranged to go out on a foursome to the cinema. My very first date was a bit of a let down. My boyfriend preferred

Christine, and half-way through the film we swapped escorts!

I went out with this young lad for only a month or so before realising we were totally unsuited. The crunch came when he took me to a Celtic and Rangers football match, but not because he was a Catholic and I a Protestant. No, it was his way with money. Poor lad, he really tried. We travelled by taxi to the football ground, but after he bought me a bar of Cadbury's chocolate and a bottle of Tizer for lunch, he was broke and I had to walk home from the Celtic ground in a borrowed pair of high heels.

He was a likeable fellow, but his failure to grasp the basics of economics frightened me. His actions closely paralleled those of Meg, when, four years ago, she had taken me to the cinema in Inverness and, having spent too much on sweets, had been forced to sell them to strangers in order to get her fare home.

I have no doubt my date did the best with a small income, but I could not understand why he had taken the taxi to the grounds. Older and wiser, I have come to the conclusion that perhaps it was impossible to get a bus to the football ground because of the crowd making its way there. Unfortunately, at sixteen I knew nothing about transport or football matches, so I passed him on to one of the other girls in the hostel.

How strange is the human mind. One night, after she returned home from a rendezvous with him, lipstick all over her face and boasting about his kissing skills, I, who had discarded him, felt jealous.

During that winter I caught a very bad flu and was delirious for one or two days. Before calling out the doctor, Miss Campbell, who lived across the road, and seemed to be involved in the hostel's administration, as well as that for a home for unmarried mothers, interrogated me in Matron's study. She demanded to know if I had been very friendly with any boys. When I said "yes," she snorted, "I thought so," and immediately left the room. It was all beyond me, and frankly, I felt too ill to attempt to analyse her apparent contempt for me.

Two weeks later, fully recovered, I was sent for by the college vice-principal. He seemed ill at ease and finally confessed he had been asked to talk to me about boys and my relationships with them. I explained that I no longer had a boyfriend, but yes, I had been very friendly with him. Obviously finding the conversation difficult, he struggled to ask what I meant by 'very friendly'. I explained that my ex, the cobbler's assistant, used to carry my books home from college on Tuesday afternoons. The poor man paled, realised he was talking to an innocent and quickly changed the subject. In the seconds it took for him to do that, I realised what Miss Campbell's "I thought so," meant. She had assumed I had had sexual relations with my former boyfriend and was pregnant.

It was my turn to be embarrassed. Would matrons and such forever intrude into my life and tell people things about me which were not true. Why? Just why? What on earth had I done to give the impression I was promiscuous?

(I had a very sketchy knowledge of sex and only a month before my meeting with the vice-principal, had advised one of the girls in the hostel that she must be aware of boys at a certain time of the month. They, I had assured her, had cycles just like us, during which they wore things called condoms. During this period they were extremely dangerous to young women. Quite how they were dangerous, I wasn't too sure, but it had something to do with giving them babies. Fortunately, the young recipient of my advice knew more about these things than I did, which explained why she treated me to a pitying smile).

The vice-principal, his equilibrium restored now that he realised I was an innocent, then asked why I did not go home for lunch. I had been spotted practising my typewriting in the classroom. I explained that as we usually just got something on toast, I did not feel it was worth the hassle rushing to the hostel and back, preferring to practise my typewriting. He gently chastised me for missing a meal and insisted I go to the canteen every lunch time and order a three-course meal for which he would pay. What a wonderful, sensitive man, but he was only one of many kind people I have met throughout my life.

Another wonderful person, to whom I was indebted, was my shorthand teacher, Miss Dow. She had a gentle character and a beautiful soft voice. I adored her. She, along with the vice-principal, helped to reinforce my belief in myself. I was not a 'bad un', I was a worthy human being and several people believed in me.

As I suspected the only reason for sending me to college was to keep an eye on me, and that my life in the hostel would not change when I left, I made up my mind to leave the hostel and rent a room the moment my studies were finished. I certainly did not wish to be like Mary, Jean or the enigmatic chemist, whose presence in the hostel baffled me. When Christine's wages were reduced by five shillings weekly after her employers bought a washing machine, we decided we would rent a room together.

When my year at college was over and I left with my seven-subject secretarial certificate safely in my hands, we found a shabby room in the West End for £1.10s per week. We paid a week in advance and put down a fortnight's deposit. Christine handed in a week's notice and I told Matron I would be leaving at the end of the week and supplied her with my new address.

On the following Saturday morning Christine and I moved into our rented room. It was one of the most exciting days of our young lives. We were on our own, master of our own fate. After returning from a shopping trip for necessities, we took another look at our finances. The provision of cutlery, china, pots and pans had proved to be a good deal more expensive than we had anticipated; neither of us had a job; our money would only last for two weeks and our knowledge of cooking and nutrition was minimal. But any concerns we had about our future proved to be futile.

At eleven o'clock the following morning, two representatives from Glasgow Corporation arrived on our doorstep. They told our landlady we had run away and they had come to retrieve us. Had my savings been greater, I would have stood up to them, but I realised Christine lacked the confrontational skills I had honed and without her I could not afford to rent the room. Reluctantly, I followed the gatherers out to the waiting car, which immediately took us to the Salvation Army Hostel in India Street.

11. My second hostel in India Street. Now demolished.

I was livid. I had given Matron my future address almost a week before; ample time for either her or the Corporation to raise their objections.

When the Corporation hauled me up to explain my behaviour, I made it quite clear that, with my father's permission, I could leave care after I reached sixteen, after all in Scotland one could marry at sixteen. The only response this assertion elicited was that Christine could not, as she 'was under a court order'. I had no idea what that meant and told my interrogator I was not Christine; my father had voluntarily placed me in care and had paid a weekly sum towards my keep. I made my annoyance perfectly clear, enunciating my words slowly and quietly, insisting I did not belong to Glasgow Corporation, or indeed anyone else.

This riled my interviewer, who now informed me that I was an ungrateful little upstart. "Have you not," she demanded, "lived in clean surroundings and had access to baths which were noticeably absent from your own house?" It was my turn to be riled. Without a second's hesitation I replied that whilst that was true, at least the water which had come out of the tap had been clean. I then stared into her hostile eyes and sweetly asked, "Are you aware that almost twenty girls are bathed in the same bath water once a week in Clyde Cottage?"

She rapidly changed the subject, demanding to know what speeds I had obtained at College. I replied that I had reached 45 wpm in typewriting and 100 wpm in shorthand. "Pretty average," was her contemptuous reply. "Not for a junior student," I replied. "Besides, we were only permitted to sit 100 wpm in shorthand; higher speeds can be obtained by sitting RSA (Royal Society of Arts) certificates at night school."

Perhaps she recalled the slave Caliban's words to his master Prospero in Shakespeare's Tempest – "You taught me language, my profit on't is I know how to curse," – because she stopped attacking me and began speaking to me as if I were a human being.

Not long after we had been taken to the Salvation Army Hostel, Christine returned up north to live with her foster parents. Although we kept in touch by letter, these became fewer as time passed. We each had our own furrow to plough.

I sometimes wonder if many of us left care unable to maintain close relationships with people because we were not allowed to communicate with anyone who had left the homes before us. (I doubt I would have met up with Christine had her younger sister not lived in the Maryhill Hostel).

People were forever disappearing from our lives never to be seen or heard from again. I believe many of us became inured to absences; took them as normal. I also believe that this policy of cutting off people from those they knew left them very vulnerable. Just imagine – no parents, no aunts or uncles and no school friends. It's no wonder so many married far too early and to unsuitable partners.

Apart from Christine, I have never met anyone I knew while in care. I did meet two girls from the Bath Street Hostel – one in London and the other on a bus to Killearn, where I had settled with my family.

It is interesting to note that most of the successful children brought up in care during my time were in the care of Barnardo's, who had a more enlightened approach, if not towards discipline, at least towards providing a career choice other than the army, domestic service or shop assistant for their children.

With help from my former teacher, Miss Dow, who bought me nylons and blue suede shoes for the event, I got an interview as a potential secretary to Mr. Dobie, one of the partners in Bannatyne, Kirkwood, France & Co., a very respectable legal firm in West George Street.

When I was shown into Mr. Dobie's office, he was sitting behind a large pedestal desk, which was littered with deeds – new ones typed on thick blue paper and bound with blue, green and red ribbon, and ancient writs, meticulously executed in copperplate handwriting. Some of them were ingrained with the dust of centuries while others, tattered at the edges where microscopic creatures had gorged their fill, testified to the transient nature of our lives.

My reflections on mortality were brought to a halt when Mr. Dobie began to interview me. I got the impression he was more afraid of me than I was of him. Eventually he announced that I had got the job and that he did not need to give me a practical test. He considered himself to be a good judge of people and their skills and he had never been wrong yet. I heaved a sigh of relief. I always found practical tests nerve-racking and sometimes failed ones I should have sailed through.

The following Monday, I presented myself at 9.15 a.m. and was introduced to the secretarial staff. There was Miss Blackwood, the supervisor, Irene who was engaged, Margaret in her mid-twenties, who was single, Laura in her late twenties who was married and Alice a young girl a year or two older than I.

It was a friendly office, with a happy atmosphere and I loved my work. At one fell swoop I had said goodbye to early starts and Saturday working. I couldn't believe my luck. My salary had also jumped to £3.10s. If not rich, I could now save and buy make-up and little luxuries. I was, I told myself, on my way.

Poor Mr. Dobie, although pleased with my work, was somewhat unnerved by my enthusiasm. He found it alarming that, before he took his hand off the bell summoning me to his room, I was there as if spirited by ghosts. I guess my lack of decorum in running up and down the stairs raised a few eyebrows.

The office, spread over several floors, was almost Dickensian, with lots of wood panelling, a few high stools for the reception area and a few open fires. Bannatyne's, at that time, was strictly a firm of family solicitors, i.e. no criminal work. Office communications were carried on with an old-fashioned courtesy, which, considering my regimented background, seemed perfectly normal to me. No first names here, except in the typing pool. Apparently, before my time, sleeveless dresses and white shoes were banned.

Standards were high. An ability to spell and type accurately was essential. Deeds were initially taken down in shorthand, drafted on to white foolscap paper in double spacing, checked by the solicitor and then transferred on to expensive blue, double-paged A3 deed paper, which meant we had to type on the reverse of two of the sheets. We were allowed one character error per page, which had to escape notice when the paper was held horizontally, and if more than three character errors occurred over the four pages, we had to start all over again. No errors were allowed in titles, addresses or numbers. Obviously three errors on deed paper could prove to be rather expensive. How easy it must be now with computer word processing programmes, which not only make it easy to correct errors before they hit the page, but also flag up spelling mistakes – surprisingly not all lawyers are good at spelling.

Mr. Dobie, himself almost Dickensian, was a plump, kind-hearted man who once told me to present myself at his wife's clothing shop in Maryhill Road, where she would happily treat me to whatever clothing I required. Needless to say, my pride prevented me from taking up this generous offer.

Along with the charming Mr. Dobie, I also worked for Miss Davidson, who had been a secretary for several years before she studied law. What she saw in me, I do not know, but she occasionally invited me to her house for supper and the theatre – either the ballet or the opera. I loved the former but, as I am tone deaf, I found the latter hard going.

Miss Davidson helped me in other ways. I did my best to hide my comparative poverty from the other girls. When winter rolled in I explained my lack of hats, scarves and gloves as being due to the fact I had been brought up in the Highlands and did not feel the cold. Miss Davidson was wise to me, and gave me a beautiful warm second-hand camel coat. The bookkeeper, Miss Gibson also gave me a lovely mohair scarf, which she said was an unwanted gift, but I knew she had bought it for me. I also pretended that I did not eat snacks in order to explain why, when everyone else was munching into a chocolate biscuit, I was not.

Although expensive purchases were beyond my reach, I upgraded my appearance. I gave myself a home perm and wore my blue suede shoes to work, but I rarely wore make-up. It fell to Miss Davidson to tell me that I should at least wear lipstick. Whatever Miss Davidson advised, I did. I idolised her. The lipstick was followed by my first pair of black, leather high heels, which I kept for best.

So far I had been more successful in finding a happy work environment than I had been in finding a boyfriend. My first, the cobbler's apprentice, had lasted for only a month or so and, apart from that short dalliance, I had not gone out with anyone else. Now seventeen-and-a-half I desperately wanted to find a special person for me. The main obstacle to this quest was my lack of social intercourse.

My second encounter with a young male took place at an end of term dance in what was probably the assembly or concert hall of the Art School. He was of medium build, blonde and very self-assured. He danced with me for most of the evening but when the dance drew to a close, instead of whisking me outside, he introduced me to three of his male friends. I felt uncomfortable as they slowly looked me up and down. I couldn't understand why they were doing this in front of him. It turned out they were going to Paris for the summer holidays and were looking for a model to accompany them, all expenses paid.

I was too naïve to understand what kind of modelling they meant and replied I thought models had to be tall and willowy. When they said they were not looking for a photographic model but an artist's nude model, I quickly explained I lived in a hostel and would not be allowed to go to Paris, let alone model in the nude. That brought my dallying with the middle class to a swift end. Without more ado, my erstwhile dance partner drove me home in his open top sports car, saw me to the hostel door, shook hands with me and said goodbye.

As no one floats in through the window, in my search for Mr. Right, I had to go out through the door. Determined to find him, I began visiting the Locarno Ballroom in Sauchiehall Street every Saturday afternoon.

Although I had a good figure and a reasonable face, I was not inundated with young men wishing to partner me. This may have been due to the fact that, at seventeen, and wearing only a modicum of make-up, I still looked like a schoolgirl. Boys on the look-out for a willing lass did not want to become involved with anyone under sixteen years of age.

My third encounter with someone of the opposite sex arose from one of my afternoon visits to the Locarno. At his request, I agreed to meet him at the La Scala cinema on the following Saturday. However, no sooner were we seated in the darkened hall than he began trying to touch my breasts, a manoeuvre I parried by sitting with my arms folded tightly over them. As I barely knew him, I was not too impressed with his behaviour.

When we left the cinema, he suggested we return to his house to meet his mother, who would make tea for us. I overrode my instincts and agreed to accompany him. I think my reservations were overcome by my desire to see inside a house – any house. However, as the bus sped out of the town towards a housing estate in the suburbs, I began to feel uncomfortable. Something wasn't right. It wasn't only the fact he was older than I had estimated which set the alarm bells ringing. Something more primal was sending out warning signals.

When we arrived at the maisonette it did not take me long to realise I had walked into a trap. No one had lived in this house for weeks, if not months. When I asked where his mother was, he replied she was in hospital, claiming she had recently fallen and was in for observation. I didn't believe him. This may well have been his mother's house but she had certainly not lived in it for some time.

12. Me showing off - "wha daur meddle wi me".

I began to feel very apprehensive and decided, should he make the wrong move, I would defend myself as if my life were at risk. I drew some comfort from the fact that my years on the farm and my subsequent daily dance exercises had made me exceptionally strong for a young woman. As previously stated, it was my proud, if somewhat unladylike boast, that I could squeeze the breath out of anyone by wrapping my legs round their rib cage and exerting pressure. I could also kick my height to the front, back and side and believed, rightly or wrongly, that if I kicked anyone under the chin, I would knock him or her out cold.

Mr. Milne had always taught me that in difficult situations it paid to keep cool; spend a few moments planning an escape route. With this in mind, and whilst my date was kissing me, my eyes searched the room for a weapon. Muscular strength was one thing, but a weapon would be more reliable. I spied a long poker lying on the hearth and slowly backed towards it with him following.

I was saved, oddly enough by the very attribute I believed kept most men at bay in the Locarno – my youthful looks. In the process of being kissed, my lipstick had rubbed off and I probably looked about thirteen years old. This threw him off balance. He stared suspiciously at me and, somewhat brusquely, demanded to know if I was over sixteen.

There was no doubt left in my mind. I was in danger. Sex with anyone under sixteen was statutory rape. I could feel my stomach churning. I did my best to hide my fear and, trying to look as if I had been caught out, stared coyly at the floor. This panicked him and within minutes he had escorted me to the bus stop. After giving me instructions on how to get home, he turned on his heel and marched off, visibly angry the prey had slipped through the noose.

It was a close call and put me off looking for a boyfriend – well for a few months.

When I reached eighteen, knowing that the Corporation could no longer legally, or illegally, order my life, with the help of Miss Davidson, I left the Salvation Army Hostel behind and moved into a hostel in Bath Street.

To celebrate the end of my relationship with Glasgow Corporation, if not hostels, she gave me a lovely pearl collar and a little card, which read "Today is the tomorrow you worried about yesterday and all is well." The pearl collar disintegrated years ago but I still have the little card safely tucked away with other little items that are of great sentimental value to me.

The Bath Street hostel was filled with a broad spectrum of girls from all backgrounds; all that is except care. At first I shared a dormitory with four other girls. It was partitioned off into cubicles containing a bed, locker and chest of drawers. For the second time in my life I had a little privacy. I was eventually given my own small room in the attic, for which I even had a key. I was in heaven. I kept my little room scrupulously clean and tidy; polished the floor until it reflected every ray of light entering through the skylight and festooned its walls with glamorous posters of Sophia Loren.

My heavy flat shoes and ankle socks were boxed and placed beneath my bed to be permanently replaced, with a few exceptions, with high heels and nylons. I had grown up.

Despite my experience with my last date, I was still determined to find Mr. Right and went to the Albert, a dance hall in Bath Street, where I met my third date. He was a totally different character from the creep I had previously dated. He was an excellent dancer and, when locked together, we literally floated over the floor as if one, with me performing steps I had never executed before. It did my self-esteem a power of good, particularly as my previous partner had, with typical Glaswegian humour, claimed he needed a driving wheel to get me round the floor!

Strange are the ways of men. It was not my youthful, curvaceous body this one was after; it was a dancing partner. In me he had found an untrained ballroom dancer who could, inexplicably, shadow his every move.

On our first date he took me to the Plaza in Eglinton Toll, a more formal dance hall than the Albert, which boasted a central fountain and tall palms. It must have been in the evening, as many of the ladies were in satin or net finery, and some were wearing strapless dresses. I'll hand it to him – ever the gentleman – he never flinched when I divested myself of my coat and appeared in my floral, cotton dress bought in a C & A sale for 15/-d. I had bought it specifically for 'the dancing' because of its voluminous skirt, which took off like a flying saucer whenever I twirled round, but, like me, it was certainly out of place in the refined atmosphere of the Plaza.

Whether it was my poor attire or my personality that put him off, I'll never know, but after he drove me home I never saw him again. This was a relief, because, apart from our ability to skim over the dance floor as light and carefree as leaves blowing in the wind, we had nothing else in common.

Finding and keeping a boyfriend was proving to be more difficult than I had thought, but my fourth was a distinct improvement on those who had gone before.

Patrick was a young, devastatingly handsome man, with black, curly hair and large brown eyes. He had everything, including the blarney. He filled every sentence with dancing, lilting adjectives and gave me that tingly, bubbly feeling I had read about in magazines. Unfortunately, Patrick was a Petty Officer in the merchant navy who spent more time at sea than he did on land, but for a few weeks he lit up my life, and that of the girls who tripped over each other to answer the door when he called.

We never went to the cinema and we never returned to the Locarno. We spent our time together driving into the countryside, parking in isolated places and cuddling and kissing non-stop. When he kissed me, my tummy did amazing somersaults and the pores of my skin seemed to want to jump from my body and merge with his. He was the first boy I ever let touch my breasts, and that only after seeking the advice of one of the older girls in the hostel, who assured me this was permissible.

Fortunately, desire was controlled by my fear of being punished by the Lord if I let anyone violate my body, and I was also terrified of becoming pregnant. Still not too sure about all the facts concerning how this happened, I was not prepared to take any chances. (While I had been in my first hostel, a young woman had passed through, presumably on her way to an unmarried mothers' hostel, and Miss Campbell had treated her with utter contempt).

Alas our trips into the countryside eventually came to an end, and he returned to his ship. I was heartbroken and had difficulty hiding my feelings from my work colleagues. At first he wrote every few weeks but then his letters tailed off. All of eighteen and not wishing to be left on the shelf, I resumed my visits to the Locarno, where I met Bob.

Like my second date, he was small and blonde, but his hair was corn yellow. During a break from the dancing, whilst we were sipping a non-alcoholic drink, he flashed a card in front of me, making sure I knew it was a driving licence. As most material things, including cars, were well beyond my means, I knew very little about them; either their cost or prevalence amongst the population. A driving licence meant nothing to me. However, when he called for me the following Saturday, and I had to climb on to the back of his 250 cc bike wearing a voluminous second-hand taffeta dress, I had reason to regret my ignorance about driving licences.

Bob was unassuming, gentle and moral. From the start, I knew I could depend on him. He would never let me down; never betray or abandon me. I had at last found my Mr. Right. He became the most important person in my life; my father, brother and boyfriend all rolled into one.

Most of our courting took place out at the Whangie, a rocky outcrop several miles outside Glasgow. Sometimes we made for Loch Lomond, where we enjoyed private picnics in beautiful surroundings. When we walked along the shores of the loch, hand in hand, skin touching skin, I would feel a beautiful warmth engulf me and would often wonder if this was how children felt when cuddled by their parents.

Touching someone who was not a boyfriend was very difficult for me, and I was well into my thirties before I could comfortably walk arm in arm with a friend, or let someone stand too close to me, particularly if they stood behind me. It seems that this is not uncommon amongst people from similar backgrounds to mine.

Another unfortunate effect of being brought up without touching or cuddling, is that many of the adults of my generation, who were brought up in care from an early age, find it difficult to cuddle their own grown-up children; cuddling adults, other than your spouse, was sometimes looked upon as a perversion! How sad. I don't accept the excuse that those who cared for us didn't know any better. At the age of eight I could spot the difference between a dog which had been patted and stroked and one which had not. If, as I have, you have ever tried to domesticate a feral cat, you will know what I mean.

Fortunately, Bob rescued me from emotional sterility. After meeting him my whole life changed. There were, of course, no changes in my surroundings, it was the inner me that began to change. My protective barrier started to crumble. I wasn't alone any more. I had a confidant. I no longer had to bottle up my innermost thoughts and hide them from people who were merely passing through my life. I could share them, hold them up for debate and in so doing learn that many of them were fallacious and destructive – many were not. When exposed to someone else's analysis, I discovered that what some called stubbornness, others called will-power. In short, I was normal – a mixture of good and bad.

On my first visit to Bob's mother in Larkhall, in order to avoid snagging my nylons on Bob's bike, I wore my ankle socks. These, along with my childish face, alarmed Bob's mother, particularly as Bob was eight years older than I was. When she subsequently realised I possessed a maturity lacking in others of my age, my relationship with her son did not seem so alarming.

There were one or two hiccups on this, my re-introduction to a normal household. When Bob helped himself to an apple from a fruit bowl and offered me one, I was shocked. Although he lived with his parents, I thought this was stealing and told him so. My next *faux pas* ocurred when I was returning from the toilet. The lounge door was closed and, before I could stop myself, I knocked on it. I recognised my mistake immediately and deliberately stumbled into the lounge, pretending I had tripped on a rug.

Poor Bob. Slowly, but gently, he taught me the difference between etiquette in homes and etiquette in houses. It was always the little things that tripped me up. Even today I can come a cropper, but today I have the confidence to laugh at my occasional clangers.

Bob and I became engaged about a year after we met. As he earned only £6 per week as a night telephonist and paid his parents £3 per week for his lodgings, my little diamond ring, costing £15, was amongst the cheapest on sale in McGowan's in Sauchiehall Street. Nonetheless, I was very proud of it and kept sticking my hand under electric lights to see it sparkle.

We threw an engagement dinner for a few of Bob's friends in the Royal Hotel. I wore a borrowed dress, coat, handbag and shoes. The menu might as well have been in a foreign language – and probably was – because the only dish I recognised was the sole bonne femme. Fish – I knew what that was and ordered it. When it arrived, covered in a white sauce, it bore no resemblance to a battered haddock or a trout fresh from one of Culantyre's rivers. "That's not mine," I piped up, "I ordered fish." There was an excruciating thirty-second silence before the waiter replied, "This is fish, madam," and placed it in front of me with what seemed an exaggerated flourish.

My mistake aside, as the night wore on, I realised I could hold my own with the guests. I did not feel the least intimidated by the fact they came from more affluent and stable backgrounds than I, nor did I feel uncomfortable because the girls were wearing outfits I could only dream about. It was beginning to dawn on me that Willie was right all those years ago when he had said "Aye, Jound, you're fit for them." And I smiled inwardly. Yes I was.

When I took Bob round to meet my Dad and to show him my ring, he showed no interest in either. Instead he went off on a diatribe against 'that one I married' who, according to him, was to blame for his poverty and he moaned that rather than waste money on such baubles, we should be helping him. He had mentioned something like this before when he had complained that I, like other children, ought to bring him bottles of whisky when I visited.

I hope these were temporary flashes of selfishness because, in many ways he was fiercely independent. It is fair to say, however, that despite receiving birthday and Christmas gifts from me, he never bought me a present or card after I left school.

Sometimes, when I look back, I think his advancing years made him realise that by spending his money on drink and gambling he had squandered away any chance to improve himself and he felt hostile to those who had not.

As Dad would or could not help me with my wedding expenses, it was therefore going to be down to me. Undaunted, I was determined I would have a church wedding and a honeymoon abroad, despite the fact the latter was a rarity in Scotland in the 1950s. There were many who thought, and some who told me, I was suffering from delusions of grandeur.

In order, therefore, to pay for our wedding, I searched around for ways to improve my income. Bob suggested I try the Civil Service. When he showed me the scales for shorthand/typists I wasted no time in applying for a post. I sat the internal examinations and after passing, was employed as a Grade I shorthand/typist with Grade II proficiencies in Springburn Labour Exchange. Overnight, my salary jumped from £4 to £6 weekly. There was another benefit, my workload was lightened considerably. This was not surprising, as a typist's output is a solicitor's bread and butter.

I also got an evening and Saturday job as an usherette in the La Scala cinema in Sauchiehall Street. Here I earned a further £2 per week, plus one halfpenny for each ice cream I sold during the interval. By now, aware that a 36-inch bust and a 21-inch waist were an asset, I made sure I showed my figure off to its best advantage during the intervals. Yip, I was learning. My strategy paid off, for it was usually the men who bought the ice creams and they preferred to come to my beckoning, illuminated tray.

No longer able to go on our beloved Saturday jaunts in the countryside, Bob visited me in the cinema. Because I missed out on my tea at the hostel, he brought, not a box of chocolates, but corn beef sandwiches.

Engaged, and my wedding date set, I felt I had outgrown the hostel and left it and rented an enormous furnished room near Blythswood Square. My landlady, an elderly, white-haired woman, belonged to the First Church of Christ Scientist, a religious order of which I knew nothing.

I found her to be strangely disconnected from the real world. After being with her for just one week she attempted to charge me for ripping one of the bed sheets. I was forced to point out that her sheets were so thin you could see through them. Confronted with the evidence, she reluctantly agreed not to charge me. In order to avoid future confrontation on this subject, I bought my own sheets.

As she rented out several rooms, I had to share the kitchen with an assortment of young people. Not too clever at commandeering the one and only cooker, and my culinary and nutritional knowledge practically non-existent, I lived mainly on fried eggs and peas, with the occasional cheese sandwich thrown in. On Sundays, I cooked mince and potatoes. Naturally, my food budget was low – all fifteen shillings of it – and I stuck to it.

During the following months, I began to collect my trousseau. I was able to buy two coats for the price of one in a small shop in the south side. For my going away outfit I chose a fitting silk beige dress and bolero, both of which were embroidered in a darker shade of beige. I had a marvellous time spending, if not wantonly, at least judicially, on pretty feminine things.

In early summer, my landlady decided to go to America for a religious conference. As she intended to be away for some time she gave me the option of leaving or paying my rent to one of her neighbours. I agreed to stay on, but told her I could not take responsibility for any of her other tenants. Before disappearing, she got rid of two of them and left two behind.

It only took a few days after she had gone for the flat to fill up with friends of the remaining tenants. They were noisy, came in late and were often drunk. If this was not enough, my landlady's departure also gave rise to peculiar behaviour by one of her male neighbours, who attended the same church as I did. A week after her departure he began leering at me across the pews. I found the look on his face disturbing but could not understand why he was behaving in this way. Soon, however, all was revealed.

One night, as I sat going over my numerous wedding calculations, I heard a car screech to a halt below, followed by the sound of a woman screaming in distress. I immediately ran to my window and saw a struggling, half-naked woman being pushed out of the car, which then took off at speed. When I recounted what I had seen to a work colleague, she told me I was living in an area frequented by prostitutes. My neighbour obviously believed, probably because of the comings and goings in the flat, that I was a lady of the night!

The following Sunday, when he persisted in leering at me, I stared him down with such a look of contempt, he never bothered me again.

Between the noise in the flat and the occasional noise in the street, I decided I must leave and Bob and I went hunting for accommodation we could share after we were married.

Most of the double rooms we looked at were ghastly. We were beginning to despair of ever finding suitable accommodation when a work colleague told me of a flat one of her friend's was vacating. The rental for the room, kitchen and inside toilet was £2.15s per week, which seemed to me to be a bargain.

Afraid the landlord might raise the rent if he thought it was for a couple, I decided to inspect it on my own and, at the same time, I also removed my engagement ring. Landlords were chary of engaged tenants, believing they did not provide security of tenure.

Glaswegians are talkative. Not only was I a Glaswegian, I was a naïve one. Mr. Paterson, the landlord, managed to elicit from me that this would be my first flat and that I had been brought up in care.

As he showed me round the premises, I could see, despite everything being covered in an eighth of an inch of grime, that all the furniture was in very good condition. The double bedroom housed a three-piece mahogany suite and matching headboard and the kitchen/living room a three-piece uncut moquette suite, a table, four chairs, an ornate cocktail cabinet, gas fire and sink. What it did not possess was either an immerser or a bath. I must confess the lack of facilities to provide hot water or have a bath did not register. Everything else to make a little home was there. I would knock it into shape.

I moved in on the following Saturday and round about 11 p.m. someone knocked on my door. As I moved cautiously towards it, I heard shuffling, mumbling and giggling. Terrified out of my wits, and after checking the three door locks had been turned, I demanded to know who was there. A slurred voice replied, "It's me. It's the landlord. I've come for the two spare pillows." Aware I had once been daft enough to enter a flat on my own with a male and thereby expose myself to possible abuse, I was determined I would not repeat the mistake.

"I'm sorry, Mr. Paterson," I replied in the most commanding voice I could muster, "I'm the tenant now and I don't open my door to anyone at this time of night." More mumbling and shuffling, but at least no giggling. Mr. Paterson apologised for inconveniencing me and he and his companion made their way down the stairs. Whether or not my openness in telling him I had come out of care, and therefore probably had no parental supervision, had inflamed his alcohol befuddled mind, I'll never know. He appeared the following morning, contrite and shamefaced to retrieve his spare pillows. I never saw Mr. Paterson again until I handed over the keys when I left.

Having calculated that I had covered all my wedding expenses with the exception of the honeymoon, which was to be funded by the sale of Bob's motor cycle, I resigned from my job as an usherette and devoted my evenings to cleaning the flat from top to bottom.

Unaware there are preparations for cleaning upholstery, I literally scrubbed the suite in the living room with a scrubbing brush and soap. It took ages but eventually it was restored to its former glory. Beneath the grime I discovered the outlines of orange and gold leaves on a beige background. For me, the worst job was cleaning the fat-filled pans and ashets stacked higgledy-piggledy beneath the sink. The previous occupant must have lived on chips.

Finally, I was able to turn to the job I enjoyed most – polishing. I wiped down the bedroom suite with vinegar; polished it until it gleamed then polished all the linoleum, throughout the flat until it shone like a mirror. I still have that passion today. Whilst I appreciate the warmth of carpets, I love to see well-polished floors.

Closer to the big date - August 30th, 1956 - and in a frantic splurge of activity, I booked the church, minister, organist, cars, wedding-cake, floral bouquets, buttonholes and corsages. I arranged for hymn sheets and invitations to be printed and bought my bridesmaid's dress. Christine, my old friend from Clyde Cottage, Dunoon, had agreed to be my bridesmaid. Unfortunately I could not afford the gold watch she chose as her gift and she had to settle for a gold locket instead.

As our wedding party was comparatively small – under twenty - I had difficulty finding rooms at an economic price for the reception. I eventually settled for the Bath Hotel, which, coincidentally, was only a few buildings away from my old hostel and had the advantage of being only a few minutes walk from the church.

13. Bath Hotel, (a few doors up from my third hostel)
where I held my wedding reception

Despite all my cleaning, Bob never shared the flat with me. When I joined the Civil Service, this gave me access to their rulebooks and their pay scales. I was stunned to learn that Bob, because of his five Highers, could become a Clerical Officer and then an Executive Officer. I urged him to apply for the Clerical Officer position. When he did so, he had been asked to list, in order of preference, which towns he would consider being sent to. He had listed Glasgow and then London (the latter because of its numerous athletic grounds).

What a Scot considered a reasonable wage, a Londoner did not.

The Civil Service in that city had great difficulty in recruiting staff, which forced them to add a London weighting on to the pay scales. Needless to say, Bob was posted to London.

Two weeks before our wedding, he was told to present himself at the GPO's offices in Charles House, Kensington on the Monday following our return from honeymoon. I had to give the landlord a month's notice, which I did a week before our wedding. This gave me a week on my own in Glasgow in which to tidy up my affairs.

Bob was neither put up nor down over his posting, but I was over the moon. With one move I would be leaving my past behind. I would have a brand new life. Meanwhile I had one task left – with only two weeks to go I eventually found a wedding dress to my taste.

On my wedding morning, I rose early and checked and re-checked my suitcase, ticking off lists of things I had arranged. Then, because Christine was hungry, I baked a mince pie and boiled some potatoes for her lunch.

As the hour of our departure to the church drew near, I hauled the zinc tub down from the toilet wall, filled it up with hot water from the kettle, stepped inside it and sponged myself down. I never regretted so much, as I did that day, the fact I had overlooked the lack of an immerser or bath when I had rented the flat.

The wedding ceremony went off without a hitch – well there was a small snag. My minister, having recently suffered a heart attack, delegated a missionary to conduct the service. He, newly returned from some foreign land, and maybe unused to this task, forgot to get us to sign the register – a fact drawn to our attention when we returned from honeymoon.

Everyone invited had turned up except my Meg. She had bought me a beautiful canteen of cutlery and her absence was puzzling. I later learned that, after buying my present, she did not have enough money to buy an outfit. Oh, but had she known, I would have gladly given her all my presents and bought her an outfit in order to have had her there. Dad, of course, faithful to himself, did not bother to buy me a present.

The excitement of the day, however, pushed these disappointments into the background. When the reception was drawing to a close, Bob and I left to catch the 7.30 p.m. bus to London. The following morning we were decanted tired and bleary-eyed at Victoria Bus Station. After a cooked breakfast, we set off to inspect the digs the Civil Service had earmarked for us.

Our room was one of many rented out by the Heigel's in Edith Road, Kensington. It was large and beautifully furnished. A portion of it had been partitioned off to form a kitchen, which, although small, contained everything we needed. It was also immaculate. We agreed to rent it, and contract signed, we spent the rest of the day popping in and out of cafes and drinking lots of coffee to keep us awake before catching the train to Southampton to board the ship waiting to take us to Dinard, France.

As the English shore became more and more distant, and the sea air whipped against my face, I leaned on the ship's railing and reflected for a few moments on my life.

I had made it regardless of my 18 moves and 8 schools, not to mention the periods not at school. Despite Glasgow Corporation's assumptions about me, at 19 I was non-smoking, teetotal and a virgin. More important, I was married to a gentle, unassuming non-judgmental man and, for all of his life, I would belong to him.

But I think Shakespeare said it better in the following sonnet:-

When in disgrace with fortune and men's eyes
I all alone beweep my outcast state,
And trouble deaf heaven with my bootless cries,
And look upon myself, and curse my fate,
Wishing me like to one more rich in hope,
Featur'd like him, like him with friends possess'd.
Desiring this man's art, and that man's scope,
With what I most enjoy contented least;
Yet in these thoughts myself almost despising,
Haply I think on thee, - and then my state,
Like to the lark at break of day arising
From sullen earth, sings hymns at heaven's gate;
For thy sweet love remember'd such wealth brings
That then I scorn to change my state with Kings.

THE END

14. Bob and I on the steps of Elgin Place Church, off Bath Street.
Now burnt to the ground!